It's Not The Money

How I Built a $2 Billion Real Estate Business Based on the Golden Rule

By Jean Burgdorff

Nebbadoon Press

It's Not The Money:
How I Built a $2 Billion Real Estate
Business Based on the Golden Rule

© 2008 Jean Taylor Burgdorff

All rights reserved.

Printed in the United States of America.

No part of this book may be used of reproduced in any manner whatsoever without written permission except in the case of brief quotations embodied in critical articles and reviews.

For information, contact the Publisher:

Nebbadoon Press

800 500-9086

www.NebbadoonPress.com

ISBN 978-1-891331-12-1

With gratitude to Gordon Imrie of Private Biographer - www.PrivateBiographer.com - who put together the original private edition containing additional family photos. This book is edited for the public and the real estate industry.

Book cover design by Leigh Zacrep
Cover photo: Burgdorff ERA Hope, NJ office

Dedicated to my children:

Charles Ferd Burgdorff
and
Peter Douglas Burgdorff

Peter and Charlie with bird and cracker, 1954.

Preface

Having some visibility in my industry, my region, and my other worlds, I'm asked for a lot of things—mainly funding! But also endorsements, speeches, jobs, tips. I enjoy responding, cultivating lives and enterprise. Also over the past several years I've often been asked, "Why don't you write a book?" When three grandchildren, Katie, Laurie, and Matthew, graduated from college in the same year, I had made a book for each of them with my favorite quotations, poems, and inspiration gathered over the years. When a colleague heard me, in a speech, refer to the book, she requested, "Couldn't you put together such a book for those of us who don't have grandchildren? Do one for us?" I've been in no rush, especially since it seems fashionable today for anyone with five minutes of fame to offer memoirs—even people at mid-life.

Though you'll soon see the sentimental aspect of this book, my great hope is that you will find it to be motivating. The world does need—as have I through eight decades—books of instruction and inspiration. A lot of parents and grandparents pass through without setting down lessons learned, wisdom received, ignorance enlightened. So I'm flattered to have been urged to record such things, and have enjoyed doing it. But you'll see from the many quotations included that I've had some splendid teachers.

I tend toward the motivational because the world, understandably, always wants to know the "Secret of Success." Of course, it's hidden in plain sight: One has to be motivated. What moves you: Gold? Or the Golden Rule? Maybe your choice will relate to what has moved me in serving and teaching, and I hope you'll enjoy and profit from my story.

∞ ∞ ∞

Table of Contents

Page vii	Preface
Page 1	Introduction
Page 5	The Big Picture
Page 11	Nice Neighbors
Page 15	Schooling and Education
Page 21	Doug Burgdorff
Page 25	Baby Boys and a Business Are Born
Page 45	Expansion, Disaster, Rebound
Page 53	Training + Bonding Make the Difference
Page 69	Ambitious?
Page 75	The Golden Rule: More Than a Tool
Page 91	Corporate Identity Breakthrough
Page 97	The First Woman
Page 101	Real Estate Industry Consolidation
Page 103	Son Peter's Homecoming
Page 115	Sale...Buyback...Resale
Page 125	Doing Well By Doing Good
Page 131	Burgdorff ERA Named #1 Company Franchise
Page 133	What Works
Page 147	Be Careful What You Wish For

Introduction

This book includes some select thoughts on success, and, of course, the world offers thousands of recipes for it. Many prescriptions are very goal oriented, and maybe that works for some people. But not for me—I never set out with real estate as a career goal, nor with a monetary target of building a company toward $2 billion in sales, beginning in my rec-room.

Maybe you can see patterns in my experience in the pages you will read. You might ask: "Jean's life has been abundant—but how about luck?" My answer is in the truism: Luck is when preparation meets opportunity. And my main preparation has been (and is) the Golden Rule. That's the pattern.

I think the Golden Rule demands trust, and trust is very difficult to define, but you always know when you have it. My trust has always been in God—Love, Truth, Principle—that's something I really know.

In my life in real estate, I have trusted God for everything. Absolutely everything. And when I speak of trust in God, I mean trust in truth, and honesty, and integrity; trust in love through compassion and unselfishness; trust in the divine Mind as the source of all intelligence.

Others have put forth useful corollaries to the Golden Rule better than I could have, so I hope you will enjoy what I collected, alongside the experiences which show the pattern. And I'm not done yet!

If I had to put it on the back-of-my-business-card, here's what's been useful to me as Life Laws:

>Going the extra mile,
>Never giving up,
>Always grateful and expressing it, and above all,
>The Golden Rule.

And from Mary Baker Eddy:

>Success in life depends upon persistent effort, upon the improvement of moments more than upon any other one thing.[1]
>
>In order to apprehend more, we must practice what we already know of the Golden Rule, which is to all mankind a light emitting light.[2]

It's a little hard to write a book about a successful life and be humble. But I feel success comes from a willingness to turn to a higher source in a childlike way. I hope some of my experiences at least illustrate that these precepts work, and can for anybody.

Love's Leading

Since Love bids you journey,
Joy goes all the way,
No moment shall weary,
No thought go astray,
Your labour is fruitful,
Your efforts are blessed
Since Love bids you journey
At Spirit's behest.
Since Love bids you journey,
The way must be clear,
Truth's glory shall guide you,
Its presence be near.
No fear shall assail you
No evil dismay,
Since Love bids you journey,
Good goes all the way.
Since Love bids you journey,
The road is not long;
Each moment is joyous,
And fragrant with song.
The desolate hear you,
And joyfully say,
"'Twas Love brought you hither,
To help us today."
     Robert E. Key[3]

∞ ∞ ∞

The Big Picture

Many good films start with an "establishing shot," and readers of this book might like one, too. Those who know me know I limit my preaching pretty much to business practices. But I was raised a Christian and became a student of Christian Science pretty early on—for reasons you'll soon understand.

Occasionally I'll refer in this book to two big books which have lit my path—first the Bible, and then another which I use as a companion to the Bible: Science and Health with Key to the Scriptures. The first has many authors, and the latter was written by Mary Baker Eddy in 1875.

Returning to the "success" point in my Preface: in Mrs. Eddy's Bible-based published writings are nearly 100 references to success and its derivatives. So obviously it was a topic of much interest to her, and she had a lot to say about it—references which have helped me understand it and perhaps even explain it. Here are some of my favorites:

> Sincerity is more successful than genius or talent.[4]
>
> Success in life depends upon persistent effort...[5]
>
> The conscientious are successful.... Be active, and, however slow, thy success is sure...[6]
>
> Success, prosperity and happiness follow the footsteps of unselfed motives.[7]

If my story might be motivating, that last quotation says it all. For years I've kept and shared a short story on "first-things first" which explains why putting unselfishness first makes sense. Its author appears to me to be unknown, but I'm pleased to see it circulates widely in cyberspace:

BIG ROCKS

One day, an expert in time management was speaking to a group of business students and, to drive home a point, used an illustration those students will never forget. As he stood in front of the group of high-powered overachievers he said, "Okay, time for a quiz," and he pulled out a one-gallon, wide-mouth mason jar and set it on the table in front of him. He also produced about a dozen fist-sized rocks and carefully placed them, one at a time, into the jar.

When the jar was filled to the top and no more rocks would fit inside, he asked, "Is this jar full?" Everyone in the class yelled, "Yes." The time management expert replied, "Really?" He reached under the table and pulled out a bucket of gravel. He dumped some gravel in and shook the jar causing pieces of gravel to work themselves down into the spaces between the big rocks. He then asked the group once more, "Is the jar full?"

By this time the class was on to him. "Probably not," one of them answered. "Good!" he replied. He reached under the table and brought out a bucket of sand. He started dumping the sand in the jar and it went into all the spaces left between the rocks and the gravel. Once more he asked the question, "Is this jar full?"

"No!" the class shouted. Once again he said, "Good." Then he grabbed a pitcher of water and began to pour it in until the jar was filled to the brim. Then he looked at the class and asked, "What is the point of this illustration?" One eager beaver raised his hand and said, "The point is, no matter how full your schedule is, if you try really hard you can always fit some more things in it!"

"No," the speaker replied, "that's not the point. The truth this illustration teaches us is: If you don't put the big rocks in first, you'll never get them in at all."

What are the "BIG ROCKS" in your lifetime? Your loved ones, your faith, your education, your dreams, a worthy cause, teaching or mentoring others? Remember to put these BIG ROCKS in first or you'll never get them in at all. So, tonight, or in the morning, when you are reflecting on this short story, ask yourself this question: What are the "big rocks" in my life? Then, put those in your jar first.

I've asked myself, "How can I be unselfish?"or, to use Mrs. Eddy's word, "unselfed?" A good answer is the advice generally attributed to Anglican clergyman John Wesley:

> Do all the good you can,
> By all the means you can,
> In all the ways you can,
> In all the places you can,
> At all the times you can,
> to all the people you can,
> As long as ever you can.

Bearing in mind that I'm by no means finished with my life's work, let's see how these aspirations play out over a lifetime.

Jean Taylor (Burgdorff), age 3 in 1927.

My grandparents, James and Adeline Owen in the 1870s.

∞ ∞ ∞

Nice Neighbors

I had no inkling of sales or managerial talent as a child. I was extremely obedient, though. I wouldn't dream of doing anything that my parents wouldn't support. If a teacher said do something, I did it. I wouldn't dream of talking back to a teacher.

I suspect I was born a music teacher. I knew from my earliest memories that that was what I wanted to do with my life. I used to teach in the basement of our home anybody who would come; if I knew two notes more than they did, I wanted to become their teacher.

In first grade I missed more school than I took. I was home, sick, all the time. I had the work brought home and my mother helped me with it.

That same year my mother was told by doctors that she had just six months to live: "Go home and prepare your husband and your child—you will be gone in six months."

A dear friend and neighbor, Florence Burgdorff, suggested to my mother, Bernice Taylor, that she try Christian Science for her cure since the medical faculty held out no hope. And my mother said, "No, I don't want to change my religion. I love my church." My mother and father were Universalists, and brought me up that way. Now the church is known as Unitarian Universalist. Mother had been an assistant to her minister in Chicago before she was married. She and my father met as young people at a Universalist conference, so the whole thing was very dear to them and they loved it.

But she decided to find out about Christian Science by sending me to Sunday School, so she allowed the neighboring Burgdorffs to take me to Sunday School. Next thing, my parents were just absolutely astounded by the fact that what had been a sickly child became a healthy child, and what had been a painfully shy child became more outgoing. And they just saw me blossom, and my mother thought, well, nothing else had changed in Jean's life so this Christian Science must have something.

Charles Edward Taylor, Jean Taylor, and Bernice Taylor, 1930.

She began to study this practical religion, and was completely healed, and lived many years after, as did Florence Burgdorff, who had made the introduction. The two families had already been friends and became much closer friends, of course, through all that. I could not stand Doug Burgdorff and his brother and sister because, unlike me, they were free spirits. And the Burgdorff theory of raising children was: "Let 'em be." We would go over to visit and I had to sit in a chair and be polite while they ran around freely—and I absolutely couldn't stand Doug.

A little girl had just finished her first week of school. "I'm just wasting my time," she said to her mother. "I can't read, I can't write and they won't let me talk!"

–Author unknown

My mother, Bernice Taylor, born 1899, in her early 20s.

∞ ∞ ∞

Schooling and Education

I was valedictorian at a New Jersey school with the double name of Scotch Plains-Fanwood High School. I didn't get many dates because I was serious, still shy, and felt I wasn't one-of-the-crowd. Also, in those days, if you were supposedly terribly smart, that didn't really attract the guys, either.

> You don't have to be great to start, but you have to start to be great.
>
> Zig Ziglar

There was one boy who was incredibly handsome (we're friends to this day) and he'd never look at me except in an intellectual situation. One day as I was running up the stairs, he was running down the stairs. He stopped, and said, "You want to go ice skating Saturday night?" I immediately said, "Yes!" I was so excited until it dawned on me when I got to the top of the stairs; I'd never even put an ice skate on, let alone knew how to skate. My dear friend Dot Lee (then Dot Tutt, who lived across the street from me and was several years younger) said, "I know how, I'll teach you."

Saturday morning, crack-of-dawn, the two of us went over to a nearby park and we started in. I was a pretty slow learner. We kept trying and trying and trying; we worked all day, and probably by mid-afternoon I began to be able to move a little bit without hanging onto her. I went home, got changed and dressed to go out with him ice skating.

I'd been trying to skate for hours and hours and hours and hours, and now my legs were so wobbly I couldn't even stand up, let alone skate! He left me sitting by the campfire while he went off skating with everybody else. At our high school class' fiftieth reunion I told that story, he was there, and he had no memory of it. It's funny, the things that stick in our minds.

After high school I went off to Boston's New England Conservatory of Music to study Public School Music Education. After two years I transferred to Columbia Teachers College in Manhattan. I was in a Masters program but I was with them for two years and I had no previous degree so I got my Bachelor's in Education.

Jean Burgdorff in high school, 1942

I studied piano at Juilliard and in my last year there my piano teacher said to me, "There is a job-opening at Rutgers University in the piano department and I think you should go and try out. Now," he said, "you won't get the job, because you haven't had any experience and you are too young," but, he said, "just the experience of trying out will be good for you."

So, I went off to Rutgers—this was the women's college. It was called the New Jersey College for Women in those days. I tried out and of course, knowing that I wouldn't get the job, I had absolutely no nerves. I played freely, talked to everybody, sight-read for them, I played two-piano music with a member of the faculty and really, really, enjoyed the time. At the end of the day they said, "Thank you very much but you are too young and you haven't had any experience so you can't have the job." And I said, "Thank you very much."

Occupation

I could never be a mortal.
They asked: What will you be
When you're a man?
When?
Don't they know? I'm about the business
Of my Father.
I take my cue from Him.
He's the I AM. I am with Him.

Donald Rain Adams[8]

Now, this dates me, but it was the end of the Second World War and in those times, the GIs coming back could study anything they wanted under the GI Bill. Have you ever heard anyone say, "I always wished I could play the piano?" All these guys who always wanted to play the piano came flooding into the Music Department. Rutgers called me up and they said, "If you will put your hair up and wear high heels, we will give you the job." Apparently that was their concept of maturity. Now I had a job teaching music in a college, which was something that I had always wanted to do! I had assumed it would be years, if ever, and many further degrees before I would have that opportunity. There I was, loving every moment of it as Lecturer in Music.

> Take a music bath once or
> twice a week for a few
> seasons, and you will find
> that it is to the soul what
> the water-bath is to the
> body.
> —Oliver Wendell Holmes, Jr.

My first pupil was a Marine who had not had time to change out of his Marine uniform. Remember, I was his age because I had been in college while he was off fighting the war. He was an absolute beginner, knew nothing about the piano. As you know, you have to do a lot of hand-work in somebody's first lesson, holding their hand and showing them the correct hand position!

I always thought I'd go on to grad school but since I got the job at Rutgers, I didn't. I taught there for four years, and during this time I was married briefly to a guy who turned out to have lied about everything. He was a total fake.

Then, Doug Burgdorff came back into my life.

∞ ∞ ∞

Doug Burgdorff

When Doug Burgdorff went overseas he hadn't finished high school. He became a heavy drinker and smoker—three packs per day—and was often drunk. When he came back from the Army

Doug in high school before WWII.

Air Service he managed to get some kind of job but it got so he couldn't take the bus to work, he'd get the shakes, couldn't hold a job, and would come home and just disintegrate from too much drinking. He told me later that when he had gone to Sunday School—it really didn't "take."

But he got one idea out of Sunday School: Life's never hopeless, that no matter what happens there is an answer. So he came to my mother, who by then had for years been a successful Christian Science practitioner (a person who helps bring healing to others through prayer). He was completely healed of smoking and drinking.

All his friends were heavy drinkers—they would go out every Friday and Saturday to the local bars and all that. So when he was healed of that, he had no friends! My mother said to me, "Wouldn't you just go out with him, just go to the movies or something, just because he doesn't have anybody?" I said, "No way!"

Remember, I couldn't stand him as a child, but finally because she wanted me to I decided to go out with him. We had such a good time! I discovered that he had a marvelous sense of humor and he was just an absolutely wonderful person underneath all this stuff I'd seen before.

Doug Burgdorff and brother Bob about 1925.

When we played ping-pong he would dive to the floor to return balls, and I thought "this is really amazing." Then he asked me to give him piano lessons and he came every night for a piano lesson. On the very day he asked me to marry him he sold his piano and never touched one again!

God said that He was going to make Adam a companion and that it would be a woman.

He said, "This person will gather food for you, cook for you, and when you discover clothing she'll wash it for you. She will always agree with every decision you make. She will bear your children and never ask you to get up in the middle of the night to take care of them. She will not nag you and will always be the first to admit she was wrong, when you've had a disagreement. She will never have a headache and will freely give you love and passion whenever you need it."

Adam asked God, "What will a woman like this cost?"

God replied, "An arm and a leg."

Then Adam asked, "What can I get for a rib?"

The rest is history....

> Author unknown

∞ ∞ ∞

Baby Boys and a Business Are Born

When Doug was healed of drinking he got a job with his friend, Ted Miller, and began rebuilding his life. Miller had opened an archery and ski shop on Route 22 in Scotch Plains named "Bowcraft." There was extra land at Ted's place, and Doug had the idea of building a miniature golf course on it.

Doug and Jean Burgdorff at miniature golf course he built, 1951.

We worked out a land lease and profit-sharing agreement with Ted, and Shady Brook Miniature Golf became a reality. Later we brought my Dad's ping pong table over to play in our quiet moments and it quickly became popular. We decided to charge a penny-a-minute and let customers play. The demand was so great Doug built additional tables until we had ten—all going strong. It was all so unexpected; we gave the proceeds to our church.

I had really loved teaching at Rutgers, but when I married Doug in 1950. I became pregnant right away, and in those days when that happened you resigned. That was just the way it was. It seems strange now doesn't it? For example, we had a salesperson at Burgdorff Realtors® years later who showed houses in the afternoon, had a buyer, went back in the evening, got a contract, signed it up about nine o'clock and went to the hospital and had her baby. It is a new era!

At any rate, I resigned, and had my first baby in 1951, Peter, who, after college, had a career in Real Estate, first with Burgdorff Realtors® and later heading up ERA Franchise Systems International. In 1952 I had Charlie. After studying at Vassar and New England Conservatory, Char-

Clockwise: Jean, Charlie, Peter, Doug in 1952.

lie had a career in child care, joined Burgorff's Information Technology department, and teaches there to this day. I did a little teaching at home but basically I was a mother and homemaker and enjoying that as well.

Charlie teaching at Summit Childcare Center in the 1970s.

Eric

He is seven and I am his teacher.
I watch him as he carefully marks each picture in
the workbook that begins with an M:
Mouse; Match; Mop.

There is a picture
of a woman kissing a baby
and I see that Eric passes it by.

He looks up at me and smiles.
"I'm finished," he says.

"What about the woman?" I ask.
His chin pushes out.
"What is she holding, Eric?"
He sighs. "A baby."

"What is that kind of woman called?"
He shakes his head
in disbelief.
"That picture is called love
and anyone who knows anything
knows that love hasn't got no M's in it."

I learn so much from Eric.

~Phyllis Rose Eisenberg [9]

Soon after I delivered Peter at home with a midwife, Doug had to go into New York City. When he came home he was just ecstatic because he had found a Norden bombsight. His job in the Army Air Corps in World War II was Norden bombsights. He had built them and repaired them and then flew with them on their missions from Italy. He had talked about the Norden bombsight but it meant nothing to me, tangibly. So he came home, I with this brand new little baby snuggled in my arms, and he said, "I found a Norden bombsight in New York City in a second-hand store and it would make a great lamp. Do you mind if I buy it?" I pictured some attractive little brass thing on which you could put a light bulb. He came into the bedroom with this huge black thing, and plunked it down on the bed, and that was the Norden bombsight!

I am so grateful that I married a man who wanted to have his own real estate business, and who asked me if I would work with him until we got out of debt. In telling our company history to a class of new salespeople at Burgdorff's, in later years one of the salespeople put up her hand and asked, "Mrs. Burgdorff, when did you get out of debt?" My reply: "Well, I'm still here."

Toddler's Creed

If I want it, it's mine.
If I give it to you and change my mind, it's mine.
If I can take it away from you, it's mine.
If I had it a little while ago, it's mine.
If it's mine, it will never belong to anybody else,
        no matter what.
If we are building something together, all the
        pieces are mine.
If it looks just like mine, it's mine.

                              Author unkown

Peter Burgdorff, age 2, 1953.

If I was a dealmaker, I learned it alongside Doug. Because I'd been a music teacher and that's what I thought I would be all my life. I had no "business training" *per se*. Doug had been a salesman from the beginning, selling home insulation, cars, and life insurance, and was extremely successful.

One day he said to me, "I think I'd like to sell real estate." Because he felt that it was the single largest investment most families make, and that it was so meaningful, he said it would be much happier, more fruitful, and a better place to be in selling homes, rather than other things.

Doug sold Fords like this one in 1955. Peter is at the right fender.

That was 1956, and in those days you had to work for somebody for two years before you could become a licensed real estate broker. He always had the dream of having his own company, and of course I was extremely supportive. So he put in his two years with a company in Summit. One day he was out driving, doing some errands, and I was out separately, also in a car. We both passed the same corner on the same day, and we both had the same idea. I came home to supper, and he said first, "I had an idea today!" and I said, "I had an idea today, too!" We had both driven by the corner, it was undeveloped, they had put a row of houses in a street behind but had left the corner open. It was cater corner from Bell Telephone Laboratories in Murray Hill. We both had the idea of building there a combination home-and-real- estate office. We paid $3000 for the lot! Must have been either early '58 or late '57.

We thought, well, it must be a right idea since we both had it the same day. Now, the only difference in our ideas was that mine was that we would build a home and office and he would have his own business. His idea was that we would build a home and office and we would have our own business. I didn't know anything about real estate and, you know, it wasn't that I thought about going into business and rejected the idea. It was that I had never thought about it, it was no part of my life experience, and I didn't expect it to be.

Doug suggested that it would be wise if I got my real estate license in that perhaps I could be helpful to him in the office. "You should get your license just so we don't do anything that's illegal." I thought, fair enough. I certainly could answer the telephone. I had learned to type in high school, so I figured I could type contracts for him and I certainly was willing to do whatever I could to be helpful.

There was no course requirement at all for getting a real estate license in those days. There was a little pamphlet about an eighth-of-an-inch thick. I studied that pamphlet, took the easiest test I ever took in my life, and then I was licensed to sell real estate in the State of New Jersey. Think of it. Industrial, commercial, whatever! There you were, supposed to be qualified to do that.

When we were opening our first office, Doug went downtown to see about getting phone service for us. He had a friend in the phone company and he thought this was going to be a snap. When he came back he said, incredulously, "They want a $1,000 deposit!" This was a lot in 1958 when we were just starting out. He asked the friend why they wanted so much, and the fellow answered, "That's in case you fail." And Doug came home to me and he said, "Fail? Fail! I never even thought of that word." It had just never dawned on him that we could possibly fail.

When Doug and I opened that first office in what would have been the recreation room in a split-level house (we lived upstairs), we made a pact with each other. The underlying philosophy of the company was this: We said we're going to look at each person who comes through the door and ask, "What can we do for them?" not, "What can they do for us?" We're not going to judge by the car they drive, the clothes they wear, how much money they have, but by The Golden Rule:

> ...Realtors® can take no safer guide than that which has been handed down through the centuries embodied in the Golden Rule. **"Whatsoever ye would that others should do to you, do ye even so to them."**
>
> ~National Association of Realtors®, Code of Ethics and Standards of Practice, Preamble

This has been a basic foundation for our business all these years. I feel that many of the people who have joined us have joined us because they shared this feeling and this ideal.

The first day we opened our doors, two families walked in at the same time. Doug took me back in the hall and he said, "You take one, and I'll take the other." I said, "I can't do that. I don't know anything!" And literally I didn't, except what was in that skinny booklet. But I really didn't know anything about selling real estate, and I certainly had not ever shown a house, but there we were. Doug said, "You take this family because they only want to see one house, and I'll take the others." I went out to the car, the people got into the back seat. People who've sold homes know that it makes you feel sort of like a chauffeur when the people get in the back.

5 Mountain Ave., Murray Hill, NJ. Our first office at right, 1958.

Then, my first panic was I didn't know how to find the house. I knew what street it was on and, as I was driving along, from the back seat came the comment, "Mrs. Burgdorff, I think we just passed the house." So I backed up and pulled into the driveway. I mention this to show how low somebody starts. No matter where our new salespeople were, they were miles ahead of where I was in the beginning.

Looking at the house I thought: "This is the ugliest house in town. You don't want to see this house, do you?" But they did want to see it. Of course the story would be perfect if they'd bought it but they didn't. However, this process continued. People kept coming into the office and I kept showing houses. I absolutely fell in love with the real estate business. I mean, I had loved teaching, but this—this was bliss. Like the first time a young couple, one on each side of me, took hold of me and said, "How did you ever find this house for us?" The highs were so high. It was so exciting, it was so thrilling, and it was so satisfying. My husband and I worked together very, very happily.

I had loved teaching and had thought I would do it all my life. But this was so much more exciting, more rewarding and more challenging. Still, I was disappointed in the public's view of a real estate salesperson. When I had answered the question "What do you do?" with "Teach music," there was interest and delight. When I said, "Sell real estate," their eyes would glaze over.

I came to have immense respect for real estate salespeople. I have always found them self-sacrificing. They work when others don't—nights, weekends, holidays. They carry their customers and clients with them in their thoughts, night and day. They get their joy from filling others' needs. They face rejection, deception, disappointment and bounce right back to try again. I resolved to devote my life to uplifting the standards of our profession—and seeing the day where we would be loved and respected. To some extent that desire has been fulfilled.

One of the first salespersons to join Doug and me was Vivian Deland. She eventually became vice president of the company. She came to us as a secretary in our office in the very beginning.

Soon my husband suggested to her that she go into selling. Vivian was a single parent at this point, and had four little children. She said, "Doug, I can't sell. I have never sold anything and I can't give up my secretarial salary." He suggested she make some calls in the evening, using the phone book, and she started to do that. Her first call, "Have you thought of selling your home?" produced the astonished response, "How did you know?" She stepped off her secretary's salary, became our star salesperson for years and years, then became a manager, and then vice president.

There are many things I really loved about our company, but two especially. One is that people came to us and achieved things that perhaps they never thought possible, and that is really thrilling to me. The second is that people tended to come and stay. We had (and have!) a lot of people with the company who had been with us a very long time and I am extraordinarily grateful for that.

In the beginning Doug went with me on every presentation so I could learn the business. My first offer was a bit low, so I timidly handed it to the owner, and sat down on the couch beside my husband. The owner angrily tossed the offer on the table and said, "I'll burn the house down, rather than take this." I got up to go, not wanting him to burn the house down. I felt a tugging on my coat from behind, as my husband pulled me back down on the couch. And two or three hours later we walked out with a signed contract and a learned lesson: "Never take 'No' for an answer."

On another occasion we went in with an excellent offer on a builder's home. We sat at the kitchen table, and he smoked a long black cigar, the smoke of which, it seemed to me, he was blowing directly in my face. Also he had only one word in his vocabulary, "No!" It was late, I was tired and I knew I was beginning to cry, so I ran out to the car. As I sat there sobbing, worried about what Doug would think, and wishing I was home with our two little boys, the front door opened, and Doug came out waving a contract. He threw his arms around me and said, "Honey, you did the right thing. After I left the kitchen the builder had said, 'Oh, I didn't mean to make your wife cry. Here I'll sign the contract.'"

I stayed in the real estate business.

Way back in the beginning, Doug and I sold mostly in Berkeley Heights-New Providence. Summit was...oh, you know, I used to go to open houses in Summit and I'd think, "How do people get to sell expensive houses like this?" It was like something out of our reach. One day a woman in Summit called up and said she wanted to list her home with us—a very large and expensive home. Doug went right over and, of course, did all the things that should be done and kind of tentatively said, "Do you mind telling me why you called us out in Murray Hill instead of using one of the prestigious Summit Realtors®?" She said, "No, I don't mind at all. Some years ago my son and daughter-in-law were looking for a place to live. They didn't have much money and they went to every Summit Realtor®, who sort of shrugged them off. They came to you in Murray Hill, and you treated them marvelously. They came home and said, 'We've found someone who really cares about us and really wants to help us.'" She said, "I decided then that if I ever got to the point of putting my home on the market that it would be with you."

I have difficulty understanding why—even if people don't have any moral or ethical or spiritual basis for using the Golden Rule—they don't just do it because it's good business. Of course they usually do use it if they have a moral, or ethical, or spiritual basis for being unselfish, caring, kind and respecting and loving the individual.

From 1958 to 1964 we worked out of the Murray Hill office. Doug handled everything to do with the business. I listed and sold properties. In 1964 Doug came home one day and he said, "There is a building in Summit I would love to buy and open as our second office. But when the

Summit Real Estate Board found out that we were planning to open this second office they passed a retroactive rule against having second offices in the same Board territory. That seems extraordinary doesn't it? Just think about the companies that have multiple offices, I mean, there are some companies, as in Morris County, that may have multiple offices within the same Board area, yet the Summit Board thought that we should not have a second one. We called the National Association of Realtors®. They said that was restraint of trade and they would revoke the charter of the Summit Board if they refused to let us have the second office, so we were able to go ahead.

> Our deepest fear is not that we are inadequate. Our deepest fear is that we are powerful beyond measure. It is our light, not our darkness that frightens us. We ask ourselves, 'Who am I to be brilliant, gorgeous, talented and fabulous?' Actually, who are you not to be! You are a child of God. Your playing small doesn't serve the world. There is nothing enlightened about shrinking so that other people won't feel insecure around you. We were born to make manifest the glory of God that is within us. It's not just in some of us, it is in everyone. And as we let our own light shine, we unconsciously give other people permission to do the same. As we are

liberated from our fear, our presence
automatically liberates others."

~Marianne Williamson
(often attributed to Nelson Mandela)

∞ ∞ ∞

Expansion, Disaster, Rebound

We didn't exactly move with the speed of light in those days. It was six years before our second office was established and another four years before we acquired our third office. One day Doug said to me at breakfast, "I think we should go west." We both laughed because "west" was Warren, New Jersey—the next town west from Berkeley Heights. We drove out to Warren and we saw a beautiful old farmhouse by the side of the road with a for-sale sign on it. Doug jumped out of the car and ran up to the door and knocked. I saw this little elderly lady (the wife) come to the door.

A few minutes later Doug was back in the car. He said they weren't able to sell it though they wanted to. They'd rented it; she told him that she was really sorry. Doug and I went to lunch up the hill and we talked and came up with this idea: we would ask her: if we found another place for the tenant, took care of all that, would she then sell it to us? And she said, "Yes." Right on the spot we made her an offer she accepted, and we drew up the contract. We got in touch with the tenant and we found another place for them to live. We had arranged the whole thing and were all set to open a third office when Doug died very suddenly Labor Day weekend in 1968. The boys were both at Pingry prep school at the time.

Charlie, Peter, Jean, Tippy the dog, and Doug Burgdorff in 1965.

At first I thought that I shouldn't go ahead with the third office, but then the people in the company, maybe less than a dozen, were so supportive. The circumstances of our finding the new site were so unusual, and sort of heartwarming, that I felt it probably was right to go ahead and open that office. And a salesperson who had just joined the company was able to go out and manage that office for us. He's still a friend.

I found myself overnight with two teenage sons, two offices and a third about to open. The salespeople met around the dining room table. There were maybe less than a dozen people with the company at that point. And they said, "We think you can do it. Let's keep the company going. We think you can do it." I appreciated their support tremendously, but I really didn't know how to run a company.

I took many courses as quickly as I could. I became the first woman CRB (Certified Residential Broker) in the state of New Jersey. I went to every national and state convention. I tried to learn as fast as possible as much as I could about running a real estate company. Doug used to get up at five o'clock in the morning and write all the checks and do all the paperwork before the phones started to ring. So I decided that's what I would do. I started to get up early, get the kids off to school, write the checks. I was still going out with every salesperson every night on presentations, so I would work all day and try to sandwich the children in there somewhere, and then go out every night on a presentation.

I think in retrospect it is probably what saved me because I didn't have any time to waste in self-pity. I was so busy trying to keep everything going I didn't have time to feel sorry for myself. Around this time Dr. Barbara Keller began providing the kind of advice which has been so fruitful for the firm.

Dr. Keller was a professor at Fairleigh Dickinson University and a tenant of ours. She had so many skills the company needed, including leading us into the computer age. She left the academic world in 1985 and came full time with the company. She has been my partner and dear friend for forty years now, and I could not adequately express my gratitude.

I'm also very, very grateful for the people who were with the company at that time who were just as cooperative and supportive as they could possibly be. We went ahead and opened the Warren office.

That third office was an obvious next step for us, although there were very few multi-office brokerage companies, particularly in New Jersey, at that point. I went to a national convention having three offices and feeling extremely proud. A California broker came over to me and he said, "Oh, how many offices do you have, Jean?" I said, "Three," thinking he'd be impressed. Then I asked, "How many do you have?" and he said,

"Thirty five." Now I realized that California, as often proved to be the case, was light years ahead of the rest of us.

Of course, you need profit to expand and serve more families. Somebody said to me one time that he felt that maybe we were too nice, and maybe we didn't care about business enough. I need to say that our emphasis on values turned out to be great for the company's value, its valuation, in fact. I learned at one point that if you are not a profitable company you are not a company. Profit is not a four letter word! It is vital, and if you don't run a profitable company then there just won't be a company. So it is imperative that we do business. It is imperative that we watch our expenses. It is imperative that we stay profitable. Most of the profits, of course, go back into services and equipment and expanding the business.

Don't Quit!

When things go wrong as they sometimes will,
When the road you're trudging seems all uphill.
When the funds are low and the debts are high,
And you want to smile but you have to sigh,

When care is pressing you down a bit,
Rest, if you must, but don't you quit.

Life is queer with its twists and turns,
As every one of us sometimes learns,
And many a failure turns about
When he might have won had he stuck it out;
Don't give up though the pace seems slow ~
You may succeed with another blow.

Success is failure turned inside out ~
The silver tint of the clouds of doubt,
And you never can tell how close you are,
It may be near when it seems so far;
So stick to the fight when you're hardest hit ~
It's when things seem worst that you must
        not quit!

Author unknown

Profit is not the goal—it is the result. If your aim and your goal are to render a service, then the result is the money comes as a thank-you. So it's really a matter of where the focus is, rather than just a fuzzy niceness goal, or not having any focus at all.

In training I naturally emphasize to salespeople that it is critical that we do business, and it is sort of important to them, too, that their own bottom line look good. I don't say, "Oh, you know, just sort of sit back and be nice to everybody and watch it happen." Salespeople need to be proactive, enthusiastic, intelligent, and show perspicacity in their business dealings.

With that approach set, good things follow. One day a young man in faded, blue jeans with holes came in and asked for our salesperson, Betty. She was out, so I offered to help him until she came back. I began asking the usual questions, "What kind of house do you want? How much do you want to invest?" To each he replied, "I don't know." So I thought I'd take him out and show him one house, just to see. On entering he exclaimed, "Oh, I love it! I'd like to buy it!" And then I thought to myself, "What have I done?" Pulling out a contract, I started with the usual questions about financing; only this time he answered, "$200,000, I'll pay $200,000," the asking price of the house. It turned out he was an author, had just written a promising book, and the publisher had given him a huge cash advance. When Betty, the salesperson, returned a little later I said, "You've just sold a house for $200,000 cash!" He lived there happily, so far as I know, ever after.

∞ ∞ ∞

Training + Bonding Make the Difference

When I started to sell, I learned everything from Doug, one-on-one. If I had a possible listing he would go with me, make the presentation. If I had a contract he would go with me, do the negotiation. When we hired a new salesperson, we did the same thing—one or the other of us would go out with him or her on every single transaction.

After Doug died, I was doing the same thing, and it meant that I was working all day, and every night I'd have appointments to go out with different salespeople. I couldn't keep that up because I had the two boys. I realized that (as the saying goes) we had to teach a man how to catch a fish, not just give him a fish, and that we really needed to do training. We started training, every time we had one or two new salespeople, then one of our salespeople took on the formal training. That's when we were doing three-to-five people at a time.

Dr. Barbara Keller

The combination of the large training room and Dr. Barb Keller joining the company full-time ignited this. She of course was an expert, with her various degrees, and she began teaching courses in listening and in personality quadrants. This was her specialty, which was really extraordinary because it helped the salespeople to know with whom they were dealing and what kind of approach those people would most appreciate. This has since become quite a common thing in other industries.

Some of the types are: Driver, Expressive, Amiable, and Analytic. Those four quadrants appreciate being treated in the way they tend to think. With an Expressive, you always ask them how they feel. With the Analytical, you ask them what they think. Barb taught this extremely helpful approach to the salespeople long before you could find it on the Internet, with slightly different shadings:

1. Driver: Give the impression that they know what they want, where they are going, and how to get there quickly.

2. Expressive: Appear communicative, warm, approachable, and competitive. They involve other people with their feelings and thoughts.

3. Amiable: Place a high priority on friendships, close relationships, and cooperative behavior. They appear to get involved in feelings and relations between people.

4. Analytic: Live life according to facts, principles, logic, and consistency. Often viewed as cold and detached but appear to be cooperative in their actions as long as they can have some freedom to organize their own efforts.[10]

One of the salespeople had just taken this course with Barb and was house hunting with an engineer. It was winter, and she found the perfect house for him, right price, etc., and she was mentally writing up the contract. As they came out the front door he said, "How do I know, with the snow, what kind of lawn is under there?" If she'd had this question before the course she might have been furious—she was an Expressive! But she knew he was an Analytic. He needed to know. She got a shovel out of her car trunk and cleared a few feet of snow away to reveal the lawn underneath, and he bought the house. There was story after story like that, of somebody who learned how to respond rather than getting upset with somebody who didn't think as our salesperson thought they should.

The salespeople, men and women, hungered for any ideas that would help them be successful. So we would bring different people in to share their expertise and we developed what was generally recognized as an excellent training program for new people. This was not what you need to get your license—that's an entirely different aspect; there are many schools which teach that.

At Burgdorff Realtors® we sort of "bottled" insight. It was well ahead of its time, and it continued to be. There were very, very few company programs for new salespeople. We became really

Jean Burgdorff at corporate HQ in 1980s

famous for that and it was one of the things that was so instrumental in our growth because people would come to us after they were licensed and want to learn, want to know what to do. The old real estate joke was, "Here's the desk, here's the phone; lots-of-luck, you're on your own!" And that was the training program of many companies. To have a formal training program, with a manual and different instructors, was very unusual.

Gifts of the Self

1. The gift of time
2. The gift of a good example
3. The gift of acceptance
4. The gift of privacy—time on one's own not smothered with demands
5. Seeing the best in people—you will see what you expect to see
6. Self-esteem—not crippling through nagging or criticizing those we love
7. The gift of giving up a bad habit
8. The gift of self-disclosure—not bottling up
9. Help someone learn something new
10. The gift of really listening
11. The gift of fun—in ordinary, small events
12. The gift to let others give to us—accept in a gracious, mature manner

Author unknown

It enabled us to hire people and arm them in ways that they might not have gotten at other companies. It was also instrumental in our retaining people because the real estate industry has a reputation as a revolving door. Having this formal training program, really made a tremendous difference.

When Barbara Keller and I came to Florida in 1999 we imported the training. It was almost a complete unknown down here. Few were doing it. It took a lot of time and effort over the years, fine-tuning, constantly refining, making changes and additions, and we still do that to this day. We brought the whole program with us and we soon developed a reputation for having this splendid training, and that was one of the ways we doubled the number of salespeople in Florida in a relatively short time.

I have always taught sections of the training program myself. I like to teach negotiation and ethics. I enjoy meeting the new people and getting to know them, being with them on a very close and personal basis when they're just starting out. It benefits them to get to know the owners of the company. And we bring in other company people to discuss other areas of expertise. At the end the new person feels like he or she knows the staff and abilities within our company.

A cardinal rule at Burgdorff Realtors® was appreciation of salespeople, customers, clients, vendors, and staff. The need for this was vividly illustrated to me one day as I walked down the hall and a secretary was approaching from the other end. As I looked at her I thought, "She handles customers so beautifully. She is such a fine person." When we came face-to-face, I said, "Have I told you recently how much I appreciate you?" Her answer rocked me: "Not only have you not told me recently, you have never told me."

What a rebuke that was! From that day on, I began looking for all possible ways to express appreciation. I always wrote a note to each person in the company for our annual dinner. This was easy when it was 20 people; harder at 100; daunting at 500, but it was the right thing to do. A small incident: I was visiting a branch office and stopped at the desk of a veteran salesperson who had pulled out of a long slump. I congratulated her, and she replied, "You know why?" She pulled open her center drawer, reached way in the back, and pulled out my note from almost a year before.

There were different ways we expressed our caring for people. The staff trips we took were tremendously unifying. It started out with Hawaii, and we took just three people! But let me tell you first about the teas.

>Ask God to give thee skill
>   In comfort's art:
>That thou may'st consecrated be
>   And set apart
>   Unto a life of sympathy.
>For heavy is the weight of ill
>   In every heart;
>And comforters are needed much
>   Of Christlike touch.
>
>   A.E. Hamilton

[My favorite poem of all time.]

We had the idea of having new salespeople come to our home for tea, and this became more valuable as we expanded. With some offices an hour away from headquarters, you wouldn't see some people in the normal course of the day. We had teas once a month. The most vivid example of wonderful response was the new salesperson who had joined the company and had come to tea. That same night she was out with her husband at an affair for attorneys, and one of the other attorneys had heard that she had gone into the real estate business, and he asked, "What company are you with?" And she said, "Burgdorff," and he said, "Oh, well, you'll probably never even meet Jean Burgdorff," in a very scornful tone. And she looked him straight in the eye and said, "Not only have I met her, I had tea with her this afternoon in her home." Flawless timing. Gave us a big chuckle.

Communication Restored

I've gone all through the day and never
    heard a word
From You, through lack of listening.

So near, yet You seemed so *far*,
The way
I've let long hours go wasting.

Nor have I thanked You.
No. Nor asked You things.
But what do You think I've learned?
How much I've missed You, Lord.

                    Thora Margaret Orton[11]

Teas were followed by monthly breakfasts for the top producers of that month, reaching a broader group than top producers for the year, and trips all over the world (Hawaii, Greece, Rio de Janeiro, Spain, Venice, the Caribbean). These trips helped create bonds and friendships not only for the salespeople but for spouses as well. The first was for five; the last, over 200. One salesperson came home after working very late, expecting her husband to be upset. He met her at the door on a cold New Jersey winter night, dressed in shorts, fins and swim mask, with tennis racquet in hand, saying, "Did we win the trip to Hawaii?"

The first Hawaii trip was in the early 70s. We took two or three of our top people to the national real estate sales convention. It was held in Hawaii, and that became a spectacular thing. With the trips and the visits to our summer place on Candlewood Lake in Connecticut, we made the business a "family" bonding experience before this became a more common thing.

Also, there were mostly women on staff in those days. The husbands jokingly called themselves the "Burgdorff Boys." The husbands of these top salespeople were so used to having their own conventions and the wives tagging along. Now they were the tag-a-longs. We found that the salespeople exchanged so many ideas when they were on these trips and there was such a bonding that there was no doubt in our minds they were worthwhile. I had a circle of business friends through membership in Masterminds, an elite trade group of independent brokers. These peers especially wondered—they were just blown away by this idea: "How do you know it makes any money? How does it affect the bottom line? You take 200 people to Italy?" It had so many wonderful effects, and these salespeople still talk about it today. I just had a phone call recently from three of them and their husbands gathered at somebody's house for Saturday night supper. They were reminiscing about the trips and they called, wanting to be in touch to say how much it meant to them and how they'd forged their friendships out of it.

> He prayeth well, who loveth well
> Both man and bird and beast.
> He prayeth best, who loveth best
> All things both great and small;
> For the dear God who loveth us,
> He made and loveth all.
>
> Samuel Taylor Coleridge[12]

The trips took a lot of planning: Hawaii, Greece. One of my people, Joann Scanlon, found Lexye Aversa, owner of Professional Touch International. The first Lexye trip was to Rio de Janiero. She was terribly conscious of the fact that we were sort of Puritan in her eyes and later she said she had told the Brazilian dancers that they had to put more on for the Burgdorff Group. They all came out in these little pasties and we didn't know what we had missed. We just thought that was it. And the "Burgdorff Boys" got a big kick out of it.

Byrd Abbott and her husband Cort on the company trip to Venice, 1994.

Jean playing donkey polo on the company trip to Casa de Campo, Dominican Republic, 1988.

Jean Burgdorff and Barbara Keller on the company trip to Hawaii, 1987.

Charlie Burgdorff and Jean Burgdorff in the Caribbean, 2003.

A faithful friend is a strong defense: and he that hath found such a one hath found a treasure.

Apocrypha: Ecclesiaticus 6:14

∞ ∞ ∞

Ambitious?

People ask me often "Did you have a Five-Year-Plan?" Or "What's your Ten-Year Plan?" I never did; in the beginning I used to be terribly embarrased that I didn't have any Ten-Year Plan. Then, many years later, I heard it promulgated at a business conference that the very best thing was seizing opportunity. And that's what I had done all along in our growth, which was, either to look for, or to be presented with—in most cases—an opportunity, and then follow through on it.

Many opportunities were like our fourth office, which was opened in Chatham, New Jersey in 1976. Faye Fischer owned the building and owned her company; she was very successful and highly thought of, and we had referred business back and forth. The Passaic River separated Chatham and Summit and it might as well have been the Euphrates because if we had somebody wanting to venture across the river we'd call Faye

Fischer in Chatham. She'd show them Chatham and we'd pay each other referral fees depending on who did what.

One day she called me and said, "Jean, I have to sell my company, my doctor tells me I can't go on and there is no one but you I want to have it." I fell for that flattery completely. I went over to see her and in one hour—bear in mind I'd never bought a company and she'd never sold a company—we had worked out the price of the building, she took back financing, we agreed on the price of the business, and we agreed on how to handle the closings which were then in process. We agreed on every detail. In one hour we drew up a very simple outline and shook hands on it. We were all set. We each went to our own attorneys and accountants and said "Here's the deal." They were not pleased that these two women had not consulted them in advance. It still worked out perfectly. She was extremely happy and so was I.

A Christmas Card Poem

I have a list of folks I know, all written in a book.
And every year at Christmas time, I go and take a look.
And that is when I realize that these names are a part
Not of the book they're written in, but of my very heart.

For each name stands for someone
    who has crossed my path sometime,
And in that meeting they've become the rhythm in each
    rhyme.
And while it sounds fantastic for me to make this claim,
I really feel that I'm composed of each remembered name.

And while you may not be aware of any special link
Just meeting you has changed my life,
    a lot more than you think.

For once I've met somebody, the years cannot erase
The memory of a pleasant word or of a friendly face.
So never think my Christmas cards are just a mere routine Of names upon a Christmas list, forgotten in-between.

For when I send a Christmas card that is addressed to you,
It's because you're on the list of folks I'm indebted to.
For I am the total of the many folks I have met
And you happen to be one of those I prefer not to forget.

                                           Author unknown

I remember the saying that women had to work twice as hard as men to match men's career advancement. I guess in the beginning the real estate world loosened up sooner for women than did so-called corporate America. (The "glass ceiling" and all that.) There may have been women who became owners of their own companies a little sooner and a little more often than in corporate America, but real estate was definitely male dominated. Ebby Halliday, a

Texas broker, may be the closest parallel to what I did in New Jersey.

But most of the women who owned companies owned more modest companies. There's one in Summit, for instance, Lois Schneider, who built what is referred to as a "boutique" company. I dislike that term, but it differentiates between the multi-office companies and a very successful one-office company. She has a substantial market share in Summit. She is a very fine woman and we're the best of friends. She never, as far as I know, either wanted to nor attempted to expand the company. Nor did I have that as a goal. When Doug and I started our company it was just the Murray Hill office where we lived and worked. Then Summit came next and I moved over my office there to manage that because you had to have a broker in each physical location.

Five-Year Plans? No. I have always trusted in growth, and this little poem explains the practicality of this approach rather well:

Trust in Growth.

"Learn to trust in growth." These were the words of
    one I sought out when my way seemed slow.
"Impatience is laziness!" she said;

"unwillingness to use the truth you know!"
The eyes were smiling that through many years
Had seen those searching comforted and freed.
"Make it a happy thing to grow," she urged.
"Persistent, patient effort will succeed."

I remember once our stopping at a farm
To buy some fruit for our dessert that night.
The farmer took us out behind the house
And pointed out a very curious sight:
Through a millstone's hole a pear tree had
      sprung up,
And as it slowly had increased in girth
It raised the clumsy, heavy granite stone
A good three feet, at least, above the earth!

Then several years went by. We stopped again
And went to find out what had come to pass.
The tree had grown, and now the prisoning rock
Was lying cracked and broken in the grass!
She paused, then said good-by and shook my
      hand
Her eyes were twinkling as I turned to go.

If there seems to be a millstone round your neck,
"Just think about the tree, my dear, and grow!"

                        Jeanette Hulst Johansson[13]

∞ ∞ ∞

The Golden Rule: More Than A Tool

Over the years, we've thrived by helping people do what they thought couldn't be done. They have dreams and we help fulfill them. When Doug and I first opened our doors we were applying that Golden Rule. If a client had trouble raising the money for the mortgage, we would loan them our commission, the money we would make on a sale. They got their home, and we got the satisfaction of being a party to it. The ethic was everywhere in the company, and I love giving examples to salespeople in my training classes.

A fellow was worn out and tired and hadn't been able to find a house. He came in the late afternoon on a hot day, and he just sank down in the chair beside my desk. "I'm so discouraged. I have to move here, I've been transferred here, and I can't find what I need." I asked him to describe what he needed. He'd been looking for days with another broker in the area. He described the house he wanted and I told him, "Well, we have it, it's right around the corner, literally." We got in my car, drove about two-and-a-half blocks, and I sold it to him within a half hour. The salesman who had been working with him for days saw me at an Open House later. He was pretty ticked and asked me, "How come you sold so-and-so a house?" I asked him, "Why didn't you sell it to him? It was right there." He looked at me and said, "I wouldn't have shown him that house. It only had a $500 commission!"

A builder had built that house and hoped to sell it himself, and had offered a token if any broker brought him somebody. He'd give $500. It would have been many thousands of dollars if it had been a resale with a full commission. The salesman was so upset. It was such a pointed lesson to me because I had never thought about the $500. I was totally focused on this poor, tired, worn-out, exhausted executive—yet there was his home. When he was transferred out again—where do you think he listed his house? And while he lived there, where do you think he sent all his friends?

A Prayer

Dear God:
So far today, I've done all right,
I haven't gossiped, lost my temper,
been greedy or grumpy, been nasty,
selfish or overindulgent.
I'm very thankful for that.
But, in a few minutes, God,
I'm going to get out of bed.
And from then on, I'm probably
going to need a lot more help.

Amen.
                                                Author unknown

Summit Interfaith Council in 1992. Jean Burgdorff was Chairman.

I know many people are not religious, some may not even be ethical, but it bears repeating: just from a pure business standpoint, the Golden Rule works. So many wonderful things happen if you do the right thing, do the unselfish thing, do the loving thing.

You Wanted a Sign?

Billboards bearing "messages from God" have appeared in at least 40 states. The wry one-liners were commissioned anonymously and devised by Charles Robb, former creative director for the Smith Agency in Fort Lauderdale. Some have criticized the signs as being too flippant, to which Robb replies, "There's no downside to what we're selling here."

The original messages, in white lettering on a black background:

1. "Let's meet at my house Sunday before the game" —God
2. "C'mon over and bring the kids" —God
3. "What part of 'Thou shalt not...'didn't you understand?" —God
4. "We need to talk" —God
5. "Keep using my name in vain and I'll make rush hour longer" —God
6. "Loved the wedding, invite me to the marriage" —God
7. "That 'Love thy neighbor' thing, I meant it." —God

8. "I love you...I love you...I love you..." —God
9. "Will the road you're on get you to my place?" —God
10. "Follow me." —God
11. "Big Bang Theory, you've got to be kidding." —God
12. "My way is the highway." —God
13. "Need directions?" —God
14. "You think it's hot here?" —God
15. "Tell the kids I love them." —God
16. "Need a marriage counselor? I'm available." —God
17. "Have you read my #1 Best Seller? There will be a test." —God
18. "Wherever you go, there I am." —God
19. "I don't question your existence." —God
20. "I'm also making a list and checking it twice." —God
21. "If we don't communicate, you haven't got a prayer." —God

---

We had a chap come in to our Middletown office and buy a house from us, and the salesperson asked the usual question, "Why did you come to Burgdorff?" He said, "I used to work for UPS. I used to go around to all the offices in North Jersey and there was a difference in how I was treated in the Burgdorff offices from the other real estate offices." He said, "It wasn't that they were giving me cups of coffee or anything. It was just that they treated me with respect. We refer to ourselves as 'brown collar workers,' and I decided that if I ever became a 'white collar worker' and had enough money to buy a house I would seek out a Burgdorff office."

He had never delivered to the Middletown office, and we probably weren't even in Middletown when he was doing his deliveries in north New Jersey, and we will never know which of the receptionists, which salespeople treated that man with the respect he deserved. That is the way we want to be: to look at each individual. Receptionists and salespeople throughout the company were following the original pledge: not "What can they do for us?" but "What can we do for them?" It doesn't matter if they have a lot of money or don't. It doesn't matter whether they are a secretary or a bookkeeper or the head of a department or a manager or in sales. Each person is unique, special, and individual, and should always be treated with love and respect by all of us. It is not just our clients and customers we are talking about. We are also talking about people within the company.

Another example: A man came into the office one day and wanted a rental. Rentals don't pay much in commissions. Some real estate companies won't even bother handling them. I did everything, however, I would do with a transferee renting or buying, showed him schools and shopping and so forth. He went back to the Midwest and called me a few days later and said he wanted me to handle the whole company's move.

He had pretended he was seeking a modest rental. He was the president of a company and he had decided on the best way to find out who could take care of his lower-echelon employees. They were coming from a modest area into the New York metropolitan area, which was much more expensive. He knew that as the president *he'd* be well taken care of. He could walk in any place and they'd kowtow to him. But he wanted to be sure his employees would also be well-served.

No other real estate office had given him the time of day. They'd give him a list, maybe, "Drive around, see what you like." So, out of that one afternoon of showing this man what he needed to see, we got the whole company! We were able to move and sell an entire company of people because one salesperson went out of her way to do the right thing for that individual. We handled all the executives and all the employees; some of them were rentals of course, but many of them bought homes. And it was such a vivid lesson to me because I didn't do it thinking,

"Oh maybe something will come from this." You just do it because it's the right thing to do. And it's definitely the Golden Rule. "How would I want to be treated if I came into an area new? What would I want done for me?" And then if you live according to that, the business just flows.

In Good Standing

Stand up—and fight for right.
    (It's just; I must)

Stand by—and still the shrill of will.
    (I'll trust)
Stand fast—and pray.
    (Above the fray,
    I'll let Love's gentle thrust
    Adjust the peace of all concerned)
    And then
Stand down
    (with meekness learned).

                    Lucile B. Leopold

Another wonderful example happened not too many years ago. A woman called our Murray Hill office and said that she would like to buy a house. Again, when asked that question by the salesperson, "What brought you to us?" she told this story: "Twenty years ago I was a young school teacher and I was not able to find a place to live that I could afford. I went from real estate office to real estate office and they really wouldn't give me the time of day when they found out that I just wanted to rent and how little I could spend."

"I came into your Murray Hill office and I poured out my story and one of the salespeople said, 'Dear, you can come and live with me until you can find a place.'" She said, "I did and I later found a place. I resolved that if ever I needed to buy a home in that area I would buy from Burgdorff." The young teacher later married and moved away. The salesperson retired and moved away. The renter was transferred to a number of different places in the United States. She and her husband were living in California when he came home and he said, "Guess what? I have been transferred to Murray Hill, New Jersey." And she said, "Murray Hill, New Jersey? I wonder if Burgdorff is still there." And of course we were still there and she bought a house from us.

As you can see, one salesperson doing a very kind, unselfish thing, twenty years later results in something happening.

...And Then Some

A retired Business Executive was once asked the secret of his success. He replied that it could be summed up in three words -"and then some."

"I discovered at an early age," he declared, "that most of the difference between average people and top people could be explained in three words. The top people did what was expected of them—and then some."

"They were thoughtful of others; they were considerate and kind—and then some. They met their obligations and responsibilities fairly and squarely—and then some. They were good friends and helpful neighbors—and then some. They could be counted on in an emergency—and then some."

I am thankful for people like that, for they make the world more livable, for their spirit of service is summed up in the three little words, "and then some."

Carl Holmes

Remember, if you do the right thing, it may come back to you, it may come back to someone else; you don't know what the results will be. But it is the way to be, and the way to act.

One day a Summit resident called and asked one of our salespeople: "I need a larger home. Should I buy a new larger home or stay and expand my present home?" After some research, our salesperson called back and asked, "Do you like your present neighborhood?"

"Oh, yes," was the instant reply. "Then I recommend you stay and add on to your present home. There are two dangers, however, in that recommendation: 1) you may overbuild for the neighborhood and not be able to get your money back, and 2) the addition could overpower the rest of the home and not be compatible with it." In this case, neither of those dangers was a factor, as there were already much more expensive and larger homes in the neighborhood, and the house could easily be expanded.

Later the owner called me to compliment our salesperson. He said, "She could easily have made thousands of dollars, but she unselfishly advised us to stay." The Golden Rule in action! And as so often happens, much business was referred to that salesperson by these people in the ensuing years.

If

If you can keep your head. when all about you
Are losing theirs, and blaming it on you,
If you can trust yourself when all men doubt you:
And make allowance for their doubting, too;
If you can wait and not be tired by waiting,
Or being lied about, don't deal in lies;
Or, being hated, don't give way to hating;
And yet don't look too good, nor talk too wise,

If you can dream and not make dreams your
    master;
If you can think, and not make thoughts your
    aim;
If you can meet with triumphs and disaster,
And treat both these imposters just the same;
If you can bear to hear the truth you've spoken
Twisted by knaves to make a trap for fools,
Or watch the things you gave your life to,
    broken,
And stoop, and build them up with worn-out
    tools;

If you can talk with crowds, and keep your virtue,
Or walk with kings–nor lose the common touch,
If neither foes nor loving friends can hurt you,
If all men count with you- but none too much;
If you can fill the unforgiving minute

With sixty seconds' worth of distance run.
Yours is the earth and everything in it.
And, which is more, you'll be a man, my son.

Rudyard Kipling

One of our salespeople had a young man from Goldman, Sachs come in, just hired from down south. He looked at properties at a moderate price level. He came back several times, and the salesperson said, "Why don't you bring your wife with you so she can see what you're seeing and help you decide?" He said, "Oh, I can't afford to, the company wouldn't pay for it, and I couldn't afford the hotel when I'm here." The salesperson said, "Bring your wife, stay in my home." He did that, and she sold him a house, of course. She told me later she directly traced $14,000,000 worth of business to that one transaction, because he told one who told one who told one throughout the Goldman, Sachs company. She wasn't thinking, "Here's Goldman, and maybe if I treat him right..." She just was a warm, outgoing, loving, wonderful person who said, "Come stay with me."

This woman, Harriet Nesbitt, was originally hired as a secretary in the Short Hills office, and her manager said to me one day, "I have to fire her because she sits at her desk and stares and listens to what all the salespeople are doing." I said. "Taffy, don't fire her—hire her!" And she became the top salesperson in the whole office and then in the whole company.

A final Golden Rule case: I was in a branch office for a gathering to honor the person who had the best sales figures for that month. During the reception that followed, a visitor came to the front door. I welcomed her, and she explained that she was a customer of a particular salesperson.

I said, "Oh, I wish you'd come a little earlier. We've just had a ceremony honoring her for her productivity. She's the top salesperson in the office."

The woman looked at me, astonished, and exclaimed, "She's the top person in the office?" I said, "Yes. Does that surprise you?" She replied, "Yes. I thought I was her only customer. She treated me so beautifully. She gave me so much time, and was always there for me whenever I called, that I thought I must be the only one she was dealing with."

That's how we've always tried to run our company, from the early days of Burgdorff Realtors® 50 years ago in New Jersey, to our ERA company today in Florida. We like all our clients to know they're important, whatever their price range.

Barb Keller and Jean Burgdorff's enthusiasm for the real estate business shows in running up to accept an award for service at an ERA International Business conference in 2006.

∞ ∞ ∞

Corporate Identity Breakthrough

In 1978, two years after the Chatham office purchase, we opened the Basking Ridge office. This we opened "from scratch," so to speak, although there was a brokerage company owner in Basking Ridge who, right after we opened, asked if we would buy his company and move to his building. I said, "I really can't do that. I just opened up a block away. How can I buy another building and move?" He said, "Well, Jean, I really want you to have my building, because I don't want it painted yellow." Yellow was our main competitor's corporate color. So, we moved into his building and it was right on the town green where it is today. It turned out to be a right move, but there was more to it than mere analysis.

> You miss 100% of the shots you don't take.
>
> Wayne Gretzky

1978 was the era of those incredibly high interest rates of 18, 19, and 20 percent. It was not an opportune time to take a major forward step in the business. At that point the company headquarters was at the Summit sales office. It consisted of Peter and me, a secretary, a bookkeeper, and maybe one or two others—a modest staff.

Burgdorff Realtors® corporate offices, 1980s.

A friend was pressing me really hard to buy his building and I decided to go to the Bible. I often would open it for a message. So I really prayed, "Is this the right thing to do?" As I opened the Bible I came right to the verse, "Be strong and of good courage, and do it." (I Chron. 28: 20.) The words were so specific, it was like they were the only words on the page, they just leaped out. We went ahead and did it, and right after we did it I got a call from a woman who owned a company in a nearby town. She said, "My partner and I and all our salespeople want to join your company." Up to that point we had used a small room on the second floor in the Chatham office as a training room, and we'd have a class of two to five people, classes of new salespeople joining the company and being trained. So here we had this new building with this huge training room. No sooner had we taken the building than we had this whole company come—and of course we couldn't possibly have had them in the former facility. It was incredible to me that there was the answer. Immediately we had the need for it and I thought right away of another Bible passage: "Before they call, I will answer." (Isaiah 65: 24)

Then we found out that when we moved what we called our corporate headquarters into this building, it transformed our company. It was something that I would never have imagined happening. I hadn't even realized we had the need. It unified the company. Up until then it had sort of been the other offices versus the Summit office and now we all became one. The Summit office had been something special because that's where my son Peter and I were.

The attitude of the company now evolved and everybody in the company looked upon the headquarters as theirs. It wasn't a "we" versus "they" situation anymore. People would come to see us or bring builders to meet us or bring possible recruits for the company, whereas they wouldn't go to a "rival" sales office. This had the effect of unifying the company and also of lifting it to a whole new level, meeting a need I didn't even know existed.

On the way back from one of my church's annual meetings in Boston I took the suggestion offered at one session to write a list of healings I'd had over my time as a Christian Scientist. I define healing as any sort of deliverance: physical, financial, human relations. I tallied 87, and my son Peter said, "Probably a whole bunch of colds and headaches." I said "No!", and then I added to my tally because I hadn't included any colds or headaches. An item on that list would have been getting the right answer on business expansion when the known facts might not have warranted it.

∞ ∞ ∞

The First Woman

I didn't set out to be a wave-maker in any sense, but I was the first woman president of the Board of Realtors® in our area. I was the first woman CRB (Certified Real Estate Broker) in the state of New Jersey. As mentioned before, I was the first woman invited to join Masterminds. All Mastermind members were major independent brokers, all had multiple offices, and they were scattered all over the US. It was a very prestigious organization, albeit all-male. They had had a broker member from New Jersey named Dick Schlott, and when he sold his company they had an opening.

One of the Mastermind members called and invited me to the next meeting, in Boston, to be looked over. The meetings always started with a big dinner. I didn't know it then, but after the dinner they would do a group photograph. So they all trooped out of the dinner and arranged themselves on the grand staircase, and I stood over at the side because I thought I was being looked over, not included. Dick DeWolfe was the president, and he said, "C'mon Jean, c'mon in the picture!" and I said, "No, Dick, I'm just here to be looked over." He said, "Oh, c'mon, if we vote you down we'll just airbrush you out!"

Single Black Female...

Seeks male companionship, ethnicity unimportant.

I'm a svelte good looking girl who LOVES to play. I love long walks in the woods, riding in your pickup truck, hunting, camping, and fishing trips, cozy winter nights lying by the fire. Candlelight dinners will have me eating out of your hand. Rub me the right way and watch me respond. I'll be at the front door when you get home from work, wearing only what nature gave me. Kiss me and I'm yours. Call 877-4160 and ask for Daisy.

(The phone number was the Humane Society's, and Daisy was an eight-week-old black Labrador Retriever.)

Date and publication unknown

The salespeople were then and continue now to be more women than men, but the owners and brokers, at that point, were all men. There still is a preponderance of men, but it's not so unusual anymore to have a woman be a broker-owner of a company. Men are still in the majority, and especially among those owning very large metropolitan-area multi-office companies, which is what Masterminds comprised. It was Dick DeWolfe in Boston, it was Wes Foster in Washington D.C., and so on. Some years later they accepted a woman from Texas. She was the second one. A bit of time passed before she was admitted.

After admitting me the Masterminds guys cleaned up their language. They did it so conspicuously that we'd be talking about something, one of them would use a four-letter word, then he'd always turn to me and say, "Oh, I'm so sorry Jean." Finally I said to them, "Guys, I may not use these words," (and I don't) "but I've heard them all and it's not like it's a shock to me to hear them." But it was interesting to me that that was their main concession to me—cleaning up their language.

At the first meeting I went to after I'd been accepted I thought, "Now, I'm going to really study up on the things guys like to talk about. I want to really be part of this group." I memorized a lot of the statistics of the ball players and what teams were ranked how, and so on, so I'd be all ready. We went out to lunch the first day of the meeting and one started to put his raincoat on and another guy came over and said "Oh, wow, that's a great raincoat! Where'd you get that raincoat? What a beautiful lining!" And then they all started to talk about their raincoats and their linings and which manufacturers they were and then I thought. "Here I am learning the baseball scores!" It was funny, I thought.

A High Goal

O Father, let me pursue excellence
So excellence be crowned, not me.
Mastery mastered in love,
And shared by all.

Then, humbly rich toward God,
Losing self and finding Life,
I find me.

Theodore L. Clapp[14]

∞ ∞ ∞

Real Estate Industry Consolidation

Masterminds is not still going in its original form. The real estate world changed so drastically and one after another brokerages or national real estate franchise systems became part of Cendant and other such large national organizations. Masterminds's rules were absolutely ironclad at that point. No one could be a franchise—Coldwell-Banker or ERA, for example, and still be a Mastermind. So the ranks shrank. In 2006 Cendant's real estate division was spun off to become Realogy, which in turn was sold to Apollo.

There was a major antitrust case in Maryland where a broker stood up in a meeting and said, "I don't know what you guys are gonna do but I'm gonna charge X percent," the government heard about it, everybody at the meeting was hauled into court, and there were heavy fines. The guy who said it, I believe, went to jail. It was really awful, but it woke up the whole real estate community to the fact that we could not discuss commission rates with each other. They gave as an example of GE and Westinghouse, who had gotten together in the early 60s and tried to fix prices on electrical equipment and light bulbs.

For Masterminds it was not a matter of setting or discussing commissions at all. That was totally forbidden. They made that rule because they were so keen on being independent, running their own show, and being beholden to nobody that they just held the line on independence as long as they could. Two of the Masterminds are now part of ERA: Jim Grandon, in the Jack Gaughen Company in Pennsylvania and Peter Hunt, in Buffalo, New York. They both became ERA brokers. Grandon sold to NRT as Burgdorff did, and Hunt maintained his independence but became a franchisee, like our company, ERA Showcase, in Florida.

Son Peter's Homecoming

By the 1980s we were making acquisitions. We acquired a company down in Fanwood-Westfield named H. Clay Friedrichs. I had known this company ever since I was a tiny child. As a matter of fact, their Fanwood office was in a little store which was known as the Corner Store when I was little, and I had spent many happy hours in that Corner Store adding stamps to my collection and buying candy for a penny and little things like that.

Ode to a Builder

I saw them tearing a building down.
A gang of men in a busy town.
With a "Yo-heave-ho" and a lusty yell,
they swung a beam, and a whole wall fell.

And I said to the foreman, 'Are these men skilled,
As the men you'd hire if you had to build?"

And he laughed and said, "Oh, no indeed,
The commonest labor is all I need,

For I can easily wreck in a day or two
What builders have taken a year to do."
And I thought to myself as I went my way,
Which of these roles have I tried to play?

Am I the wrecker who walks my town,
Content with the labor of tearing down?
Or am I the builder who works with care
That my town may be better,
      because I've been there?

                    Author unknown

Both my boys, Peter and Charlie, had lived with real estate. One night at dinner they said, "Could we just have one dinner without real estate talk? One!" This was when they were in high school. Peter had gone off to college later and done other things elsewhere. It never dawned on me that he would come back and join the company, and it seemed even less likely that Charlie would. Then, Peter called me one day and said, "I'd like to come back and join the company." I was absolutely thrilled. After being a salesperson for a period, he thought he would like to work with builders. He handled that very well. We would buy a piece of property, retain a builder, and then would sell the home and land, making our profit from the land and the sale.

Nathan, Arom, and Charlie Burgdorff, 2004.

The Cold Within

Six humans trapped by happenstance
    in black and bitter cold
Each possessed a stick of wood,
    or so the story's told.

Their dying fire in need of logs,
    the first woman held hers back
For on the faces around the fire
    she noticed one was black.

The next man looking 'cross the way
    saw one not of his church

And couldn't bring himself to give
    the fire his stick of birch.

The third one sat in tattered clothes
    he gave his coat a hitch,
Why should his log be put to use
    to warm the idle rich?

The rich man just sat back and thought
    of the wealth he had in store,
And how to keep what he had earned
    from the lazy, shiftless poor.

The black man's face bespoke revenge
    as the fire passed from his sight,
For all he saw in his stick of wood
    was a chance to spite the white.

And the last man of this forlorn group
    did naught except for gain,
Giving only to those who gave
    was how he played the game.

The logs held tight in death's stilled hands
    was proof of human sin,
They didn't die from the cold without,
    they died from the cold within.

       James Patrick Kinney

We enjoyed working together—I was, of course, happy to have him with the company—but it is not easy to work for your mother! And we wrestled with titles, one of the harder things we did. One of the hardest things for him was, if he did something, I got the credit, because I'd been there for so long. He was walking down the street in Summit one day and one of the businessmen said, "Peter, this new program that you have that your mother started is so great!" And it was Peter's program, totally! He thought of it, he started it, he initiated it, he ran it. So that was one of the harder things, to be sure that he got credit and had a good sense of his own worth. It was very heartwarming because for years he was "my son." When he later became President of ERA International, I was known merely as "Peter's mother." He had a period of really coming into his own, which was good. But before all that, Peter was the president of the company when sales went over $1 billion and got to join the "Billionaire's Club."

Glynis and Peter Burgdorff, President of ERA International, on a trip to Banff, 1998.

Before that Peter had an opportunity, because he had started our mortgage company, to join a national mortgage company, Equitable Mortgage in Clearwater, Florida. Equitable offered him the chance to travel and present corporate mortgage programs to corporations, which was very appealing. He also thought Equitable would allow him to see if he could, in fact, be successful without just being the son of Jean Burgdorff. Up until that time I had just sort of assumed that he would take over my company one day and that's the way it would be. All of a sudden he wasn't there.

The salespeople were kind enough not to say, "Well, you are so old that maybe we are going to need someone else around here." They did say things like, "What if you got hit by a truck? What would we do?" This was also a time when

Peter Burgdorff and young daughter Julia (behind wheel). 1992

the national real estate companies were coming into flower—Merrill Lynch, Better Homes and Gardens, Sears—they were all out there, they were all looking for companies, and all wanting to acquire. We were, in fact, courted by most of the major national firms.

I was very reluctant to sell the company, partly because I felt that the name Burgdorff had come to stand for something. Not just that it was my name, but I felt we really stood for something in the real estate community which was special and very ethical, so I hated to give up the name. With most of these buyouts you must give up the name. There were other reasons, of course, why I didn't want to sell. There was a lot of pressure from within the company and so I felt that probably it was the right thing to insure the continuity of the company.

Self-control and Grace

Few would deny the importance of self-control. Not all, however, link this quality with grace. But self-control reveals grace in a meekness and wisdom unknown to the garrulous talker, unexpressed by the self-willed worker. In the perceptive words of the poet Emily Dickinson,

> Capacity to terminate
> Is a specific grace.

"Capacity to terminate"—to recognize the very moment at which to stop some activity and actually to reveals self-control and Expresses a vital aspect of grace. The necessity for terminating some wrong activity is obvious. Not so readily apparent is the need for temperance and judicious timing of legitimate action. Mary Baker Eddy, who discovered and founded Christian Science, once ended an extemporaneous talk on the subject of timeliness with this thought-provoking statement: "The right thing done at the wrong time is no longer the right thing" (Mary Baker Eddy; A Life Size Portrait by Lyman P. Powell, 1950 Edition, p. 221).

Willingness to stop one right activity to make way for another of more immediate consequence is an essential part of right timing. When one is due at work, for instance, legitimate home duties and even prayerful study are not excuses for tardiness. It is right to be at work on time; and however worthy some home duty may be, if it makes one late for one's job, it becomes "the right thing done at the wrong time."

Gracious dominion is gained step by step as one seeks God's guidance not only for the right start but for the correct ending of an activity. Acknowledging the ever-presence of God-governed action, one gains wise control in major and minor situations. For example, one learns to leave a good book at the very moment duty calls, to terminate a cherished social contact in time to lend help to another, to stop in the midst of legitimate correspondence when something more important demands attention. Self-control is found through the under-standing that God's man reflects divine wisdom and judgment, which render impossible even the slightest degree of over activity in any direction.

Character traits which hinder right timing can be overcome through the understanding that right control is inherent in man's true nature, through the recognition that God's perfect government of every action is never dormant, never interrupted. In her book "Retrospection and Introspection," Mrs. Eddy points out these certain demands made on each of us (p.79): "Be temperate in thought, word, and deed. Meekness and temperance are the jewels of Love, set in wisdom. Restrain untempered zeal."

Take one of the obvious enemies of right timing— conceit. The conceited individual fails to make way for another's words or acts, fails to stop at the right moment. The vain conversationalist continues too long, assuming unflagging interest on the part of his listeners. The egotism which impels one to be garrulous or aggressive diminishes when one grasps the undeniable fact that God enables all His children to express Christlike love. Endeavors to manifest self-control are not fruitless when supported by the clear recognition that God's man, always prompted by the wisdom of unselfed love, cannot overdo any aspect of activity. The truth is that divine intelligence guides and controls him continually. Because God's every action is perfect, unassailably wise, man in God's image cannot, even for a moment, manifest a conceited determination to persist.

Take another enemy to right timing—self-will. Linked with unbridled desires, blind to spiritual wisdom, self-will incites one to push on merely because one wants to. Temperance and self-will are never allies. When self-will is at the root of stubborn persistence to carry on beyond the right stopping point, one needs the grace to listen to God's guidance—the humility to realize that this guidance may sometimes come through the advice of a relative or a friend.

Knowing that God's man is always obedient to His will, one gains the ability to yield graciously to the promptings of divine Principle. Christ Jesus said (John 5:30), "My judgment is just; because I seek not mine own will, but the will of the Father which hath sent me." God's purpose for man is always right.

Acknowledging divine Mind's control and acting on this basis, one learns to free himself from willful overaction. Through the recognition that God's will is always done, one learns to obey Principle at every point. ...

The Christian Science Monitor[15]

∞ ∞ ∞

Sale...Buyback...Resale

In 1986 a friend of mine in Connecticut called up to say, "Jean, I just sold my company to a bank. They are absolutely wonderful! They went public. They have lots of money. They are paying money up front." Most of the other companies would pay out as-you-went, but they were paying up front. He said, "They let you keep your name and they let you run your company. It's really the best of both worlds—just incredible! I thought, "Ah-ha, perhaps this is the answer."

Decisions Before Their Time

How few things demand an immediate decision. I may think that I have a decision to make, but I find that often this is not so at all. The ongoing flow of my experience, if I am attentive to it, has a way of clarifying things which at first might seem obscure or confusing.

> Many times, tomorrow has shown me that yesterday's "decision" was an illusion. Thinking that I had to decide something was just a misguided effort on my part to try and shape an event that was not ready to be shaped. Does a caterpillar sit around trying to decide whether or not to be a butterfly?
>
> Alex Noble[16]

I quickly got in touch with them, met with the gentleman from Center Bank, and we did, in fact, structure a buyout. Peter came back to new Jersey and assisted with negotiations to sell the company, but left on December 31, 1986 upon the sale to Center Bank. They gave me a five-year contract. Though we became a wholly-owned subsidiary of the bank, they said I could run the company. They put right in the contract that we could keep the "culture of the company." They had a lot of money, they wanted to invest it, and they wanted us to expand. Now, I had never had the opportunity of expanding with OPM (Other People's Money). We'd used our own personal funds or what we could borrow from somewhere, so this was a whole new experience also. Consequently, we acquired quite a list of offices rather quickly.

As the president of the subsidiary I was invited up to Connecticut to sit on their board, and at the very first board meeting the president of the bank made quite a statement about something that he planned to do and then he said, "I want everybody's advice—what do you think about this?" Nobody budged. Guess-Who, of course, put her hand up? I gave my statement of what I thought of what he said, the good points and the danger points and what we should think about. There was this dead silence in the room. After the meeting one of the guys came over to me and said, "Don't ever do that again!" I said, "Do what?" He said, "Don't ever, ever offer your opinion on what he said! Don't ever do that." But then I realized that the president had asked for everybody's feedback, had gotten none, and apparently it was because he didn't want anybody's feedback. They all just sat there in absolute silence.

The Greenest Light

When something is right for me, I always have an indescribable sense of peace about it. Knowing that this sense of peace is available as a guide and criterion gives me a great sense of confidence regarding decision. If I am considering a course of action, I look closely at the feelings that this prospect evokes. Is there a sense of pressure, compulsion, confusion? Is there a desire to have the approval of others, even though I may be acting against my better judgment? Is there a fear that unless I act, I will lose an important opportunity? Reason and logic alone rarely offer final guidance, although they can be extremely helpful in bringing to light the various factors I need to consider and be aware of. It is this one simple question that always leads me to the answer: "Do I have a sense of peace about this?"

Alex Noble[17]

One of the main things the Center Bank wanted was to grow the company. That was their mandate. And we had the cash to do it, with OPM (Other People's Money). One company we bought had three offices, another had three in Hunterdon County, and most of the others were one-office operations. At the point of the Connecticut bank's purchase of Burgdorff Realtors®, our growth became exponential.

But we began to have a feeling that things were not exactly the way we would like them to be in our relationship with the bank. They had said when they acquired the company that they were aware it was a cyclical business. Unfortunately the 1987 through 1989 cycle was a down cycle, as it was for the bank too. By the fall of 1989 Center Bank had decided that purchasing real estate companies was a mistake and began actively trying to sell the real estate companies it owned. The company they bought in Connecticut went down first, because Connecticut experienced the recession before New Jersey did. But then we began to experience it also and the bank got very cold feet—they were just beside themselves. They didn't know how to handle it at all. Their first reaction to it was to fire the president of the bank. They put a man in charge who was very fine, and he and I got along very, very, well, but the business did not improve, and so they fired him. They put another vice president in charge and the business still did not do too well, and they fired him. So then, at the end of three months, a fourth chap was in charge and I will just say that he and I did not have the same standards, or methods, or whatever, and I real-ized it was not working.

The Bridge Builder

An old man, going a lone highway,
Came, at the evening, cold and gray,
To a chasm, vast, and deep, and wide,

Through which was flowing a sullen tide.

The old man crossed in the twilight dim;
The sullen stream had no fears for him;
But he turned, when safe on the other side,
And built a bridge to span the tide.

"Old man," said a fellow pilgrim, near,
"You are wasting strength with building here;
Your journey will end with the ending day;
You never again must pass this way;

You have crossed the chasm, deep and wide-
Why build you the bridge at the eventide?"
The builder lifted his old gray head:
"Good friend, in the path I have come," he said,

"There followeth after me today
A youth, whose feet must pass this way.
This chasm, that has been naught to me,
To that fair-haired youth may a pitfall be.

He, too, must cross in the twilight dim;
Good friend, I am building the bridge for him."

      Will Allen Dromgoole

Peter and I had long discussions about buying the company back. We decided it was time for Peter to be president of the company and I to be the chairman: Peter would own the company.

The motivation for the buyback was to preserve the culture of caring for the individual and the ethical basis of the company. My five-year contract allowed me to preserve that culture until the last day of 1991. It was clear to me that the culture would change dramatically after my contract expired and I was gone.

Peter and I made an offer in late 1989 to purchase the company back from the bank. The bank rejected the offer out of hand. Nevertheless we continued negotiations, with Peter as the lead negotiator for two more years. Every time we thought we had an agreement with the bank, they would add new demands.

In 1991 we hired a business broker to try and pull it all together. In November we closed the deal on almost the same terms we originally offered in 1989. This two-year period was the most difficult negotiation either Peter or I had ever experienced. In retrospect, we are grateful that it took so long, as it was simultaneously the bottom of the real estate market. The company started to be profitable just before Peter bought it back.

Remember, the bank had given me a five-year contract ending in 1991. We closed on the buyback just before my contract was expiring. The chap whom they had put in charge said, "Well, Jean, are you aware that your contract is expiring?" I said, "Yes, I certainly am." He said, "You know, if we hadn't worked this out, I was going to come down and run the company." I was particularly glad that we had arranged the buyout because I cared a lot about the company.

I will only say one thing to show you the difference. He had no regard for salespeople. He felt that salespeople were expendable. "Oh, you lost some? Get some more." I knew what it meant to have salespeople join the company. I realized how special, how precious and indispensable they are! I have often said that if our offices and all staff in them, including me, disappeared overnight there would still be a Burgdorff Realtors®—a strong company. If the salespeople disappear, we don't have anything! We don't exist to send memos to each other. We exist to have the salespeople doing business for us.

The best salespeople recognize advantages and disadvantages to every market. Let us fastforward to 2000, for example. We had eight offers on a property, all higher than the asking price. That's one happy seller, one happy buyer, but seven disappointed clients. In a slower market, people have more opportunity to look around. When mortgage interest rates hovered around 18%, you could still succeed if you thought creatively. Anyone with motivation, spirit and stamina can weather any market. People who can't be flexible will drop out.

As the old man walked along the beach at dawn, he noticed a young woman ahead of him picking up starfish and flinging them into the sea. Finally catching up with her, he asked why she was doing this. She answered that the stranded starfish would die if left until the morning sun. "But the beach goes on for miles and there are millions of starfish," countered the old man. "How can your effort make any difference?" The young woman looked at the starfish in her hand and threw it to safety in the waves. "It makes a difference to this one," she said.

Author unknown

In retrospect 1986 was the absolute peak of the market. The year that I sold the company was at the very top of the market. I received all sorts of credit for knowing that it was the peak and that it would go down. Of course I did not know that—I had no idea. I thought things are getting better all the time; they will always get better all the time. I did not have any sense it was not going to continue that way. You may remember that 1991 was the absolute bottom. After that things started to turn up again. In 1992 our sales went over the billion dollar mark. When we bought the company back and there was a turnaround, again I received wonderful credit for knowing exactly when to sell the company and when to buy it back. I had no idea, no idea at all but I was, of course, grateful that that had happened.

Five years after the 1991 buyback, when we sold it the next time, to Cendant's National Realty Trust, everybody was saying, "When another five years is up, will that be the year we buy it back?" No, by 2001 it was too large and we couldn't possibly afford to buy it back.

∞ ∞ ∞

Doing Well By Doing Good

A Christian Science church in Maplewood, New Jersey called me and said they wanted to sell their building. I had some qualms about how you would sell a church. It was beautifully designed and it was historic. I had a good friend who was an architect. I said, "Come with me and just look at this place, without any limitations—just tell me what you think as you step inside, what could it be?"

I was thinking of making it into maybe two or three condominiums because there were several very large buildings in the older towns in New Jersey where that had been done. They made quite nice homes for people and had a nice piece of ground around it, but it was too much for one person, so they'd divide them into condominiums. That was as far as my thinking had gone.

We went into the building and he looked around, and he said, "Oh, Jean: theater! It's a theater." We both laughed because we knew that was impractical. There was no way we were going to be able to do that. He had some other ideas too, so I decided to call a meeting of the neighbors and talk to them about how they felt about this building and what they'd like to have happen in their neighborhood.

The Burgdorff Cultural Center. 2008

We got the neighbors together in the church, and I just kind of bared my soul to them. I told them I wanted it to be something that would be a blessing to the neighborhood, that they would like, and here were some of the ideas. And I told them what this architect had said. I said, "But, of course, that's completely an impossibility." And one of the men put his hand up and said, "Unless, Mrs. Burgdorff, you donate it." And then everybody laughed!

> The fragrance always remains in the hand that gives the rose.
>
> Heda BeJar

I got to thinking about it later, and I thought, "Why not? Why not?" So, I did. They named it the Burgdorff Cultural Center, and the town operates it. The Recreation Department takes care of who can have it when. The first thing that happened was that the local drama group, called The Strollers, linked to the place. They do excellent, excellent productions. They had been going from pillar to post, they'd be in a school for one play, then they'd be in a building for another; so this became their home. They could keep their props there, they could keep their costumes there, they could do their rehearsals there. They were ecstatic about it.

Then one thing after another unfolded. Concerts were the next thing, then children's programs, and it just got so there was hardly any time that it was dark. They were just producing one wonderful thing after another. The church property included a sort of mini-library and bookstore on the main street adjacent to this, and that became the Maplewood Burgdorff Realtors® office. From a business standpoint, because the name Burgdorff was received happily and gratefully by the people in town, that was a great blessing to our office. It was not the original motivation of it.

Similarly, Mildred ("Millie") Robbins Leet and her husband Glenn, when vacationing in the Caribbean, came up with the idea of an international "trickle up" non-profit organization. They were very concerned about the poverty that they saw. They realized that so much private and governmental aid targeted for people at the poverty level was siphoned off and didn't get to the people that really needed it. Americans normally think of "trickle" as trickle down when it comes to economic matters. The Leets wanted to put forth the idea of aid going to the very lowest level of poverty and thereby trickling up through the family, the community, and the world. The organization they founded was named Trickle Up.

As Trickle Up's website declares: "Trickle Up empowers people living on less than a dollar a day to take the first steps out of poverty, providing them with resources to build microenterprises for a better quality of life. In partnership with local agencies, we provide business training and seed capital to launch or expand a microenterprise, and savings support to build assets."[18]

Most of her beneficiaries are Third World women—but indirectly this, of course, helps feed kids, husbands, and communities. I built one business: Trickle Up has helped start or expand 150,000 businesses!

Two days before a big dinner honoring Millie, her assistant called to ask me to give a toast to Millie. I woke up in the middle of the night and I thought, "Proverbs!" (chapter 31). You know, "Who can find a virtuous woman?" And as I read it every verse that I read was Millie Leet, and her beneficiaries, and it ends up, "Give her of the fruit of her hands; and let her own works praise her in the gates," (which, of course, is exactly what's happened with Millie). "Strength and honor are her clothing...she reacheth forth her hands to the needy."

I turned out to be the last person to speak. I stood up in front of this very eclectic combination of New York and United Nations people, and I said, "Do you all know that there's a chapter in the Bible written about Millie Leet?" Then I read it. You could have heard a pin drop. They all just became so quiet. And they practically cheered at the end. Millie was sitting there with tears running down her face. It was just absolutely perfect for Millie.

Burgdorff ERA Named #1 Company Franchise

This abridged trade-paper article from *Realty Times* by Blanche Evans is a fair snapshot of the company by 1998:

> Peter Burgdorff must feel as good as a proud papa. After becoming sole owner and president of his parent's New Jersey realty company, Burgdorff Realtors®, in 1991 he expanded staff and sales by more than 25 percent, breaking the $1 billion barrier in one year. By 1995, Burgdorff Realtors® ranked 34th in the nation in dollar volume. In 1996, Burgdorff Realtors® became an ERA franchise, and Burgdorff went on to become the president and CEO of ERA Franchise Systems, Inc. Meanwhile, Burgdorff Realtors® continued the momentum he began. Burgdorff Realtors® is now the number-one ERA franchise worldwide.
>
> That is a significant achievement out of over 2,600 offices in over 50 states and 18 foreign countries. Burgdorff Realtors® achieved an

outstanding $1.75 billion in sales and more than 6,200 transactions.

"This is an extraordinary honor," says Judy Reeves, president of Burgdorff ERA. "I am extremely proud of every member of our sales team. Because of their hard work and dedication, as well as the unflagging loyalty of our clients, 1997 was our best year in history. It is doubly exciting because this high award comes during Burgdorff's 40th anniversary year, so we have a lot to celebrate and a great deal for which we are grateful."

Burgdorff ERA has more than 600 associates and 30 offices across New Jersey and Eastern Pennsylvania. One hundred and sixty-two of the associates and branch office managers earned a four-day, expenses-paid trip to the Las Vegas ERA International Convention earlier this month, where the company announced Burgdorff ERA's achievement.[19]

What Works

Something that constantly delights me is that selling real estate—especially residential properties—provides an opportunity for women, in particular, to use qualities that are natural to them.

I don't exclude men, of course, but in my experience, qualities such as intuition, empathy, and enthusiasm often come so readily to women. And I can think of several other qualities, natural to men and women alike, that make the selling of real estate a joy for seller and buyer—unselfishness, compassion, patience, integrity, honesty, caring, listening. You don't need a lot of formal education to develop these qualities. They just need to be practiced on a day-to-day basis. Bringing out the best in our salespeople inspires loyalty. And that flows two ways—to and from employer and employee. When I find someone working 100 hours a week, I like to think they're not doing that just to impress me, or because of the money they hope it'll bring. I hope that person's committed to a principle—and that that's what they're being loyal to.

Our company has never been famous as a "revolving door." And I like to think that those who have stayed for 20, 30, and even 40 years have not done it so much out of personal loyalty to those of us in charge, but out of loyalty to the principles that we try to espouse.

These principles aren't just written on a piece of paper; they aren't just in the policy manual; they aren't just talked about at meetings. We've really pledged ourselves to live them every day.

Yes, it's unusual to have employees who stay with a brokerage for as long as many have at Burgdorff. Many people come into the business, don't last, and go out, or go to another brokerage firm. There are some more factors which, in combination, work for us.

One is trying very hard to only hire people whom you feel quite convinced are going to be successful, because your entire business reputation rests with each one. It's transaction-by-transaction and it's one-on-one. You hire someone, they become the company to the world. Somebody comes in and they deal with "Ann"—

they don't think of it as dealing with Burgdorff Realtors®, and Ann can either make or break the situation depending on how she handles people.

So all through the years people have asked me over and over and over and over and over and over again "What did you look for in hiring?" The answer is complicated, but one thing I always asked myself when anybody came looking to work for us was, "Would I want to buy a house from this person?" If there was anything—if their eyes were shifty, or if they talked too much, or anything that made me feel no, I wouldn't trust them—then I wouldn't hire them. But if I felt a strong appeal, even though they didn't know anything about selling real estate yet—if I felt that people would like them and trust them and want to do business with them—I'd hire the applicant.

In employment interviews I looked for people who could tell you an event or an experience in their life that demonstrated confidence or success. People have said, "I sold Girl Scout cookies and I sold more than anybody else." Well, that's a definite sales mentality. If there's anything that they've done that they're proud of, that's a good indicator.

It was a combination of endeavoring to hire that kind of person and then training, of course, not only in classes, but one-on-one, and with your entire life focused on that, continuing it—not just a preliminary training. On our Florida brokerage website Barbara Keller and I are listed right there as trainers. Barb teaches the personality quadrants, interpersonal skills, and listening, and I teach time management and negotiation. We do it for several reasons: 1) to really know the people who are joining the company, 2) to know them very well in that relatively small class environment, and 3) get them to know us, what strengths we may have that they can call on in their career. You could call it "active mentor-ing," since the salespeople don't have to chase us to get trade secrets.

The World Is Too Much with Us

The world is too much with us; late and soon,
Getting and spending, we lay waste our powers;
Little we see in Nature that is ours;
We have given our hearts away, a sordid boon!
This Sea that bares her bosom to the moon,
The winds that will be howling at all hours,
And are up-gathered now like sleeping flowers,
For this, for everything, we are out of tune;
It moves us not. – Great God! I'd rather be

A Pagan suckled in a creed outworn;
So might I, standing on this pleasant lea,
Have glimpses that would make me less forlorn;
Have sight of Proteus rising from the sea;
Or hear old Triton blow his wreathéd horn.

William Wordsworth

In selling real estate, no one gets paid unless the client's needs are met. Realtors® are not paid by the hour; they're not paid by the job; they're just not paid unless they're successful in selling a home on acceptable terms, or finding a home that truly meets a buyer's needs. That makes meeting the customer's needs the priority, with the dollars earned coming as thank you or reward. I've always taken the broadest possible view of home. There are walls, bathrooms, kitchens, fireplaces, and so on, but one of the most important things is location—the surroundings, the people next door, the neighborhood, the community, city, state, whatever.

I realized early on in my real estate life that I couldn't pretend to know exactly what was right for somebody else, because the implications of that decision went so far beyond a physical structure. I remember a time when my husband and I bought a house that was OK, but certainly not thrilling. Yet it turned out to be one of the best moves of our lives, because our backyard was adjacent to the backyard of another family, who brought so much richness into our lives. Their children became very close friends of our children, and that's gone on now to the third generation, with their grandchildren now baby-sitting for our grandchildren.

On top of having that broad view, real estate is a kind of work where you must be self-disciplined, a self-starter, be able to work without anyone standing over you saying, "Do this and do that." Some people find that very difficult. The characteristics we seek are not learned in school. Have we ever been stunningly wrong? Never in the sense of someone "doing us in," but there was one case I recall, the first time I had to fire somebody.

This young man was very handsome. He came in every day and did nothing: read the paper, drank coffee, and talked to other salespeople. I knew I should fire him but I had just taken over the company after Doug died. I had never fired anybody, nor hired anybody. Doug did all that business, the check-writing, the money-borrowing, the hiring, the firing. I just happily sold properties.

I knew that this Greg had to go, and every day I would come in and every day I would get cold feet and would not do it. One morning I opened up the Bible for an answer, and it opened up to the verse in John 11:39 that says, "Lord, by this time he stinketh for he hath been dead four days." I thought, "Boy, you couldn't have a clearer piece of guidance than that!"—I walked in the door and Greg was there. Before I could open my mouth he said, "Oh, Jean, I've gotta see you right away." I said, "Yes, I want to see you too," and he came back in my office and said, " I have the best news: my wife is pregnant!"

Well, my fallback position had been that his wife had a good, excellent salaried job and my getting rid of Greg was not going to endanger anything because his wife made the money in the family. Now his wife was pregnant but I knew I had to do it anyway and I said, "Greg, I think that's wonderful but you're fired." (I did it a little differently than that, but basically that was it.) He packed up his stuff, he left, and about an hour later my secretary came in and said. "It's Greg's wife on the phone." I wanted to tell her I wasn't there. I didn't want to talk to her, but picked up the phone. She said, "Jean, I want to thank you. It was not the right thing for Greg. He's not self-disciplined and a self-starter, he was in the wrong place, and I just want to thank you for having the moral courage to do that." He went out and got a nine-to-five job and did well.

> Do not say things. What you are stands over you the while, and thunders so that I cannot hear what you say to the contrary.
>
> Ralph Waldo Emerson

There've been other bad hires. It's very difficult to tell if somebody is really going to be successful. We look for enthusiasm, energy, empathy, intelligence, trust. It's hard to know in an interview. Over the years and especially in the early days I would talk my friends into coming into the real estate business because I would say, "This is wonderful, this is heady, this is better than anything I ever thought existed, this is thrilling, you've gotta be in the business!"

Sometimes I would have an intuition. I remember when a young woman came in to be interviewed for a secretarial job. After ten minutes with her I said, "Go into sales." She seemed horrified: "I've never sold anything in my life!" Remembering my own introduction to real estate, I said, "Neither had I." That was Shirley Bentley, who went on to become one of our best salespeople, and saw more success in the business after she had to move to Cape Cod.

One of the friends I persuaded to come into the business had six children. We were very close friends and our two boys were very close friends of two of their six. She said, "Jean, I can't sell anything, I never sold anything in my life." She was very quiet, and dressed conservatively, spoke softly. But people knew that what Trudy said was the truth. She was absolutely dependable, absolutely trustworthy, absolutely without prevarication of any kind. She was just wonderful. She did marvelously well and she said, "When the sixth child graduates from college, I'm resigning." So she sold for several years, put all six children through college, the sixth one graduated and she resigned, just like that.

One day we were sitting on the dock at our Connecticut summer-place, where we took salespeople a lot. We were sitting side-by-side and Trudy looked at me and said, "I taught myself to swim." I said "What?" She continued, "When I was a little girl, my parents would not let me go near the lake where we lived. They would not let me take swimming lessons. I was determined to learn to swim. So I went every day, sat by the side of the lake and listened to the swimming lessons, and when all the kids and instructors went home I got in the lake and I practiced what I had overheard, and taught myself to swim." I looked at her and I said, "Trudy, that's it." That's the quality that gave her the total determination to succeed in whatever she set her mind to doing.

You can't put motivation in anybody. It has to come from within. You can teach skills, and you can reinforce; but you can't make someone want to do something.

This came to mind in the case of an impending speaking engagement, when I suggested to my hosts "What in the world would I have to offer to the Christian Science Visiting Nurse Association, never having been a nurse?" she answered: "You've just been so successful."

One former nurse I knew was Mary Lou Spillane, who, sadly, drowned not long ago at the New Jersey seashore. She was a salesperson and an absolute delight. She had a terrific sense of humor. The people who were nurses make marvelous salespeople—they're so caring and devoted to other people's well-being. She worked in our Short Hills office and was immensely successful and became a dear friend, as most of my salespeople did.

To succeed, you must care about people and their desires, needs and wants. If you're reading this and were to consider work in this field I obviously love, here's one way to test yourself: if you have a meal at an excellent restaurant or read a good book, do you share your experience and enthusiasm with your friends? The need to share the things we like and appreciate is the essence of our business. If you can't stand rejection, don't think about going into this business. Flexibility is another quality you must have. You will be working when most people are off. One needs unselfishness, determination, persistence, and kindness. The perfect real estate agent must also have what I call "the fire within."

You have to want to find the right property for your client, to put together the deal that meets your client's needs. You make friends and you learn people's dreams, not just the financial details of their lives. Deep friendships develop and they last. When you work with people through the purchase of their first home, you have the opportunity to work with them through all the stages of their lives.

Here's some feedback from all those hiring decisions I have done over forty years: I received a rather large box recently and when I opened it up it said "Jean's Birthday Box," and in it were cards, letters, poems, from dozens and dozens of people at Burgdorff. The word got out somehow that it was my 80th birthday—I was trying to keep it sort of under wraps. Somebody discovered it and they all knew about it and sent this box. It was so thrilling. I worked my way through dozens of cards and one of them had written me a poem. She wrapped it around a bag of chocolate. I took the poem out and left the chocolate in the box. I thought "I'll eat that later." Later came. I took the chocolate out and there were fifty more cards underneath the chocolate that I had thought was just wrapping!

I tell this tale because one of the cards was from our marketing director at Burgdorff when I left nine years ago. We had a very pleasant relationship. I respected him, and I felt he respected me, but there was no close connection, as you sometimes have. It was very polite, and I have no bad words at all about him. And here comes this essay from him.

He wanted me to know how much I had meant to him, how much he had learned from me, that every time I spoke (presumably at meetings, not just everyday) he just felt he grew so much because of it, it made such a difference in his life. Well, with some people I would have thought, "Yes, indeed, thanks a lot," but I was amazed this man was writing this way!

The sale of Burgdorff Realtors® in 1996 was followed by a stint of three years under contract with Cendant, after which I was free to look for my next opportunity. It came over lunch with Peter when he said "Mom, I'm about to lose one of my best franchises in Florida." This was followed by a filial nudge and "unless, Mom, you'd like to buy it," and he laughed. I had never thought of buying another Real Estate company but the idea clicked. "Don't laugh Peter, that's a great idea!" So Barb flew us to Florida and we bought "Showcase Properties and Investments" and a condo and a car, and flew home to prepare to enter a new experience.

Barb and I agreed to switch roles: she would be President and I would be Vice President. Showcase was a fraction of the size of Burgdorff, so Barb and I anticipated an easier life of moderate business involvement interspersed with tennis and swimming. WRONG!

Jean Burgdorff and Barb Keller at their new plane in 2006.

It took our full commitment just as Burgdorff had and it has grown to ten offices and 150 salespeople plus a title company and a major Property Management Department. It still thrills us to be #1 in our Brevard County marketplace, and to win numerous awards in our overall ERA rankings.

∞ ∞ ∞

Be Careful What You Wish For

"But Jean," I hear you asking this, "What about money? Isn't success about having a lot of money?"

Management expert John C. Maxwell put it well. He believes there are "two basic paths to achievement a person can choose. You can go for the gold or you can go for the Golden Rule."[20] There are many people out there who have gone for the gold and who appear to have achieved all life has to offer. But haven't we all noticed that appearances of ease and comfort can be deceiving?

Dear Child:

Good Morning!

I am God. Today I will be handling all of your problems. Please remember that I do not need your help. If you come across a situation that you cannot handle, DO NOT attempt to resolve it. Kindly put it in the SFGTD (something for God to do) box. It will be addressed in MY time, not yours. Once the matter is placed into the box, do not hold on to it or attempt to remove it. Holding on or removal will delay the resolution of the problem. If it is a situation that you think you are capable of handling, please consult me in prayer to be sure that it is the proper resolution. Because I do not sleep, nor do I slumber, there is no need for you to lose any sleep. Rest my child. If you need to contact me, I am only a Prayer away. Your loving Father-Mother,

God

Back in the mid-70s I was in the middle of a meeting when someone came in and announced, "It's all over: Sears is going into the real estate business." It wasn't all over. Sears lost a pile of money and went out of real estate.

Merrill Lynch made a foray into the business, but couldn't make stockbrokers into real estate agents.

Without Internet marketing, a laptop and a Blackberry a salesperson will be behind the pack in this race, but there is one unchanging fundamental. It's a one-on-one business. It is all about one person listening to another and caring, searching for the right property, negotiating the deal, arranging financing, and helping them realize their dreams.

The Garment

She wears old age like a gown
not her own –
a hand-me-down
more than second-hand –
something to relax in at the end of the day.
Of course, you understand
it's just the dress that's out of style,
with seams awry, and buttons sprung.
Herself is young,
in a private, special way all the while.

Laura Baldwin

Grandmother Adeline Owen in her 80s serving as a volunteer in 1958.

People (or organizations) who go for the gold often trade everything else of importance in their lives for the chance to grab it.

Here's a true story of Howard Bowen, who stuck with the Golden Rule instead of the gold. Howard was responsible for the construction of many Kmart stores when the department store chain was at the height of its success. And it made him highly successful.

That road wasn't always easy. When Bowen was working on landing the first contract with Kmart, he went down to Florida to look at sites. After touring the area all day with two representatives from the corporation and some others, one of the executives, who had a bad reputation, suggested that all of them go to a strip club. Now Bowen had a dilemma. The deal he was trying to win was worth $40 million. And he knew that if he didn't go along with this man's request, he could jeopardize winning the contract. But Bowen believed in practicing the Golden Rule, and he knew that going to a strip club would be a betrayal of his wife.

He summoned all his courage and asked to be taken back to the hotel before the group went out that night. "I'm sorry, but I just can't do it," he told them. "Besides, I really need some rest."

As they pulled up to the hotel's entrance, Bowen got out of the van. That's when another one of the people who had been riding with them said, "You know, I really need to get some rest too," and he also got out of the van. Then another did. In the end, nobody went out that night. Later, the executive who had originally made the suggestion told Bowen, "You have no idea how much I respect you." He also awarded Bowen the contract. Is a person who maintains his integrity always rewarded in that way? Of course not. But what if Bowen had compromised his ethics and still not won the contract? Then he would have had neither the revenue nor his self-respect.

Bowen was an advanced thinker. Some hard questions he asked in his 1950s book, *Social Responsibilities of the Businessman*, should be asked today. And how grateful I am that the Golden Rule has steered me around these very real pitfalls:

- "Should [the businessperson] conduct selling in ways that intrude on the privacy of people, for example, by door-to-door selling...?"

- "Should he use methods involving ballyhoo, chances, prizes, hawking, and other tactics which are at least doubtful good taste?"

- "Should he employ 'high pressure' tactics in persuading people to buy?"

- "Should he try to hasten the obsolescence of goods by bringing out an endless succession of new models and new styles?"

- "Should he appeal to and attempt to strengthen the motives of materialism, invidious consumption and 'keeping up with the Joneses' "?

And in case you find Bowen's tale of "turning them around" in Florida a bit remote, hear what happened to my husband Doug: One morning when he was a car salesman (before real estate, but after he was healed of drinking alcohol) his sales manager took a group of them into Manhattan to an automobile show. His first stop was at a bar. They all got out and followed him, lining up at the bar. The manager ordered liquor and so did each one in line. Doug was the last, and he ordered a ginger ale. Whereupon the salesman next to him said "Oh, cancel my drink, I'll have ginger ale, too." And so it went down the line until the manager was the only one having liquor. Later the other guys thanked Doug for his courage.

None of this is to suggest that successful people are ethically challenged more than the rest of us. But success in the world's terms is not what makes us necessarily memorable or influential in ways that, deep down, we'd prefer. An anonymous little test I clipped years ago worked its way onto the Internet and I hope is provoking "Ah-ha!" thoughts around the world:

Quiz:

1. Name the five wealthiest people in the world.
2. Name the last five Heisman Trophy winners.
3. Name the last five winners of the Miss America contest.
4. Name ten people who have won the Nobel Prize.
5. Name the last half dozen Academy Award winners for best actor and actress.
6. Name the last decade's World Series winners.

Now, take another quiz:

1. Name three teachers who inspired you to achieve in school.
2. Name three friends who helped you through a difficult time.
3. Name five people who taught you something worthwhile.
4. Name three people who made you feel appreciated and special.

5. Name five people with whom you enjoy spending time.

6. Name half a dozen heroes whose stories have inspired you.

My whole family was together at Christmas 2007 for the first time in a long time. Top row: Charlie, Chris, Doug, Julia, Simon, Nathan, Peter. Middle row: Barb, Katharine, Arom, Glynis. Bottom row: Victoria, Matthew, Jean, Laurie, Dave. The new additions included my great grandchild Victoria, Laurie's husband Dave, and a friend from Australia, Simon.

∞ ∞ ∞

Endnotes

[1] *Miscellaneous Writings 1883-1896* by Mary Baker Eddy, p. 230, The Christian Science Publishing Society, Boston, MA.

[2] *The First Church of Christ Scientist, and Miscellany* by Mary Baker Eddy, p. 282, The Christian Science Publishing Society, Boston, MA.

[3] *Poems* by Robert E. Key. Gloucester, UK: John Bellows, Ltd., 1947.

[4] *Message to The Mother Church, 1900,* by Mary Baker Eddy, p. 9, The Christian Science Publishing Society, Boston, MA.

[5] *Miscellaneous Writings,* by Mary Baker Eddy p. 230, The Christian Science Publishing Society, Boston, MA.

[6] *Miscellaneous Writings,* by Mary Baker Eddy p. 340, The Christian Science Publishing Society, Boston, MA.

[7] From an article by Mary Baker Eddy, A10260, and is reprinted courtesy of The Mary Baker Eddy Collection, The Mary Baker Eddy Library for the Betterment of Humanity, Boston, MA.

[8] By Donald Rain Adams. Reproduced with permission from the September 26, 1977 issue of the *Christian Science Sentinel* (www.cssentinel.com). ©1977 The Christian Science Publishing Society. All rights reserved.

[9] By Phyllis Rose Eisenberg. Reprinted with permission.

[10] Copyright ©2004 Steven Wille. www.toughteams.com/papers/4-quadrant.htm

[11] By Thora Margaret Orton. Reproduced with permission from the May 1, 1990 issue of *The Herald of Christian Science,* French Edition (www.leherautsc.com). ©1990 the Christian Science publishing Society. All rights reserved.

[12] From *The Rime of the Ancient Mariner.*

[13] By Jeannette Hulst Johansson. Reproduced with permission from the January 1955 issue of *The Christian Science Journal* (www.csjournal.com). ©1955 The Christian Science Publishing Society. All rights reserved.

[14] By Theodore L. Clapp. Reproduced with permission from the August 24, 1981 issue of the *Christian Science Sentinel* (www.cssentinel.com). ©1981 The Christian Science Publishing Society. All rights reserved.

[15] Reproduced with permission from the November 8, 1963 issue of *The Christian Science Monitor* (www.csmonitor.com). ©1963 The Christian Science Publishing Society. All rights reserved.

[16] By Alex Noble, Reproduced with permission from the July 6, 1979 issue of *The Christian Science Monitor* (www.csmonitor.com). ©1979 The Christian Science Publishing Society. All rights reserved.

[17] By Alex Noble, Reproduced with permission from the September 19, 1980 issue of *The Christian Science Monitor* (www.csmonitor.com). ©1980 The Christian Science Publishing Society. All rights reserved.

[18] www.trickleup.org

[19] Reprinted with permission. Burgdorff Names #1 Company Franchise by Blanche Evans. *Realty Times*, 3-25-98. ©1998 http://RealtyTimes.com

[20] By John Maxwell, Reprinted with permission from *There's No Such Thing as "Business" Ethics*. Grand Central Publishing.